Interactive
BIBLE
Bulletin Boards
Summer

by Susan Julio
and
Cindy Schooler

These pages may be copied.

Permission is granted to the buyer of this book to reproduce, duplicate or
photocopy these student materials for use with pupils in
Sunday school or Bible teaching classes.

Rainbow Publishers

Rainbow Publishers • P.O. Box 261129 • San Diego, CA 92196

✳ Dedication ✳

To my family: Our 3-year-old, Caroline, who is my inspiration and guinea pig; our 16-year-old, Josh, who is my encourager and artist; and especially Marvin, who is and has been my mentor, sage, counselor, best friend, cheerleader, soul mate, husband and pastor for the past 20 years. Thanks, Sweetie!

— C.S.

INTERACTIVE BIBLE BULLETIN BOARDS FOR SUMMER
©1998 by Rainbow Publishers
ISBN 1-885358-35-0

Rainbow Publishers
P.O. Box 261129
San Diego, CA 92196

Illustrator: Joel Ryan
Editor: Christy Allen
Cover Design: Stray Cat Studio, San Diego, CA

Scriptures are from the *Holy Bible: New International Version* (North American Edition), copyright ©1973, 1978, 1984 by the International Bible Society. Used by permission of Zondervan Bible Publishers.

Printed in the United States of America

✸ Contents ✸

Interactive BIBLE Bulletin Boards

✳ Introduction ✳

Bulletin boards can be fun, involve your students and use easy-to-find supplies, plus look great and offer solid Bible-teaching. That's why *Interactive Bible Bulletin Boards* was created: to provide the materials you need to make bulletin boards that you can use to teach about God. Each of the four seasonal books in the *Interactive Bible Bulletin Board* series contains 13 bulletin boards for preschoolers and 13 bulletin boards for elementary-age kids. Just one book has enough bulletin board patterns and ideas for your church's entire children's department!

The best part about this book is that all of the bulletin boards either involve the children in creating them—allowing you more time to spend on teaching—or involve them with learning manipulatives that you display. Either way, you will quickly construct exciting bulletin boards that reach kids.

Each bulletin board is a lesson, including:

✳ Plan	the lesson's objective
✳ Memorize	an age-based memory verse
✳ Gather	a supply list
✳ Prepare	pre-class tasks for you to complete
✳ Create	step-by-step instructions
✳ Teach	ideas to extend the lesson

You will also find all of the patterns for each bulletin board, plus borders and lettering to complete the board's look. Tips on pages 6-9 will help you make the most of the book, as well as your supplies and creativity.

The bulletin boards in this book are unique. They were created out of a desire to see children using the bulletin board as an extension to teaching a biblical concept. These boards say, "Yes, please touch" in a world that tells children, "No, don't touch." The children in your classroom will love the new experience you are about to give them.

* How to Create Beautiful Bulletin Boards Using the Materials in This Book *

Each of the 26 Bible-teaching, interactive bulletin boards in this book contains complete instructions, patterns, lettering and borders to put the bulletin board together, plus teaching hints to use the board with your class. The following pages will offer you ideas for your bulletin boards and explain how to best use the book.

* Backgrounds

Each bulletin board in this book includes suggestions for background colors—most people use poster paper or construction paper. You may want to select a background that will work with board designs you will use throughout the season. Also, feel free to experiment with materials of your choice to add background interest, such as:

- * Textured fabrics: felt, flannel, burlap, fur, cheesecloth
- * Paper or plastic tablecloths
- * Gift wrap
- * Cotton batting
- * Newspaper
- * Brown paper bags crumpled and then flattened
- * Maps
- * Crepe paper
- * Colored tissue paper
- * Wallpaper
- * Self-stick plastic in colors or patterns
- * Shelf paper
- * Colorful corrugated paper available from school supply stores
- * Poster board on which figures may be permanently attached

* Making Bulletin Boards Three-Dimensional

Although bulletin boards are normally flat, there are many imaginative ways to add a three-dimensional effect to them. Many of the bulletin boards in this book already include ideas for three-dimensional effects, but there are others you may want to try:

* Place cork, cardboard or foam behind figures or letters.

* Attach large figures to the bulletin board by curving them slightly outward from the board.

* Glue or attach three-dimensional objects such as cotton balls, pieces of wood, twigs, nature items, feathers, yarn, toys, small clothing objects (like scarves and mittens), balloons, artificial flowers or leaves, chenille wire, fabrics, corrugated paper, sandpaper, crumpled aluminum foil or grocery bags, rope, plastic drinking straws—the list can go on and on!

✳ "Stuff" figures by putting crumpled newspaper or paper towels behind the figures before attaching them to the bulletin board.

✳ Flowers may be made from individual egg carton sections by cutting off the sections and painting, coloring or decorating them as desired.

✳ Heavy objects may be mounted in the following way: Cut two or more strips of bias binding tape or ribbon (available from fabric stores). Securely staple one end of the bias tape to the bulletin board, place around the item to be mounted and staple the other end (above the object) to the bulletin board so the object hangs securely on the bias tape strips.

✳Lettering

This book includes full-sized lettering which is intended to be used on the bulletin boards that you create. To use the lettering, you may do the following:

✳ Trace the lettering onto colored construction paper, cut out each letter and mount them individually on the bulletin board.

✳ Duplicate the lettering onto any paper. Then place that page over the sheet of paper out of which you want to cut the letters. Cut through both sheets using scissors or a craft knife. Mount the letters individually on the bulletin board.

✳ Duplicate the lettering onto white paper and color in the letters with markers.

✳ Duplicate the lettering onto white or colored paper. Cut the words apart and mount each word on the bulletin board in strip form.

✳ Trace the lettering onto paper of any color using colored markers. Cut out the individual letters or cut apart the words and use them in strip form.

✳ Cut the individual letters out of two colors of paper at once. When mounting the letters on the bulletin board, lay one color on top of the other and offset the bottom letter slightly so it creates a shadow effect.

Attractive lettering can also be made by cutting letters out of wallpaper, fabrics, felt, self-stick plastic in colors and patterns, gift wrap, grocery bags, newspapers and other materials. For a professional look, outline letters with a dark marker for a neat edge and good contrast. Always try to use dark colors for lettering, unless the background requires a contrasting color.

Textures may be used for lettering also, either by cutting the letters out of textured materials or by gluing on glitter, sequins, straw, twigs, yarn, rope, lace, craft sticks, chenille wire or other materials.

To mount the letters flat, staple them to the board, use double-sided tape or roll a small piece of tape to make it double-sided. Always put the tape under the letter so it does not show.

Stagger the letters, arch them, dip them or make them look like stair steps or a wave by variegating one letter up and one letter down. Be a non-conformist when it comes to letter placement! Curve your lettering around the board, place your title down one side or across the bottom. Your title doesn't always have to be across the top of the bulletin board.

✳ Duplicating Patterns and Lettering

All patterns, lettering and borders in this book may be used right out of the book or traced, enlarged, reduced, duplicated or photocopied to make your bulletin board.

The easiest way to duplicate the materials in this book is to use a copy machine to simply copy the patterns, lettering or borders onto white or colored copy machine paper. For a nominal price you can copy onto colored paper at most copy centers. Construction paper works well in some copy machines.

You may also trace the materials in this book onto white or colored paper by holding the page you wish to trace up to a window or by using carbon paper.

Another way to enlarge items is with an overhead projector. Trace the items you wish to enlarge onto a transparency sheet, then project the image onto a sheet of paper attached to a wall. Adjust the projector until the image is the size you desire and trace the image onto the paper.

✳ Mounting Materials onto Your Bulletin Board

It is important that all materials stay securely on your bulletin board until you wish to take them down. This book does not specify how to mount most materials so you may choose the method that works best for your situation.

Stapling materials directly to the bulletin board is the most secure method of mounting most materials and the staples are virtually unnoticeable. Be sure to have a staple remover handy both when you are creating the board and when you are taking it down.

Staples are much better for bulletin boards for small children as it is quite difficult to pull a staple out of a bulletin board, unlike push pins and tacks. Make certain that no loose staples are left on the floor after you finish working on the bulletin board.

Pins may be used if you wish to support the materials rather than make holes. Double-sided tape, or tape rolled to make it double-sided, is also effective. For heavier materials, use carpet tape or packing tape.

✳ How to Make Your Bulletin Boards Durable and Reusable

Cover both sides of your bulletin board figures—especially those that will be manipulated by the children—with self-stick plastic. Cut around the figures, leaving a ¼" edge of plastic. (If one figure is made up of several parts, put the parts together before covering with plastic.) You may also glue figures to colored construction paper and cut around them, leaving a narrow border of construction paper.

Also laminate the captions and borders to use again. Take a picture of your completed bulletin board for future color references and diagrams. Glue the developed picture to the outside of a large manila envelope and store the laminated pieces of the bulletin board inside.

✳ Teaching with the Bulletin Boards

Each of the bulletin boards in this book includes a suggested memory verse and teaching tips to help you use the bulletin boards to teach important biblical concepts to children.

On those that are designed for the children to assist you in the board's creation, you will find that the students delight in helping and seeing their work on the board. The boards that you create for the children to use in learning will also intrigue and engage them. Almost all of the boards that the children will help you to create require scissors and a few other easy-to-obtain items. A list of materials is included with each board.

Since the titles for these bulletin boards were chosen to encourage a learning concept, they are important to the overall interaction with the bulletin board. The first week that each new bulletin board is displayed, read the titles aloud to the children—especially preschoolers—and explain what it means. Also, show the children how to interact with the board. If you take time at the beginning of the class to introduce the board, you won't have as many individual questions to answer during your lesson. Memory verses were purposely not included on most of the finished bulletin boards for preschoolers since they cannot read, but your continued verbal repetition of the verses will make them familiar to the students.

Bulletin boards are great teaching tools. Besides being obvious colorful additions to a classroom, they can also be used in the following ways:

* Reinforce the lesson
* Improve fine motor skills
* Serve as the focal point of classroom
* Review the previous week's lesson
* Introduce new topics
* Encourage new skills (such as following a maze, turning wheels, opening flaps, etc.)
* Keep and encourage attendance
* Enhance self-image by displaying work
* Encourage interaction with other children

These bulletin boards are unique because they encourage the children to interact with them in some way. Whether the board displays their own work, helps record attendance or allows them to move objects around, the children are encouraged to interact with the bulletin board each time they come into the classroom.

* Visitors

Be sure to create a few extras of each child-specific item so that visitors will have copies. Your new students will feel more welcome if they know you are prepared for them.

* A Special Note to Preschool Teachers

The best way to organize a classroom for toddlers is down on your knees! Remember that these are little people, so make sure all of your displays are at their eye level. Lower the bulletin board if possible. Make sure the children can easily reach the interactive activities you create with this book.

✳ Borders

Borders are the frame of your bulletin board. Just as you carefully choose an appropriate frame for a picture on the wall, you should choose a border that will enhance your bulletin board. Several border patterns are provided on the following pages for use with selected bulletin boards in this book.

The easiest method for creating and duplicating borders is decribed below. Simply measure the top, bottom and sides of your board (write down the measurements so you will have them the next time you are making a border). Then follow the directions for instant borders. Cut, fold and trace as many strips as you need for your board based on your measurements. You may use colored paper for the borders or copy the patterns onto white paper and have the children color them in with markers.

Glue or tape the border lengths together. Use double-faced tape to attach the border directly to the frame, or staple the border to the edge of the bulletin board. Roll the border to store for future use.

Attractive borders may also be made with the following materials:

* ✳ Artificial flowers, leaves or nature items
* ✳ Rope or twine
* ✳ Braided yarn
* ✳ Wide gift wrap ribbon
* ✳ Corrugated borders from school supply stores
* ✳ Twisted crepe paper streamers
* ✳ Christmas tree garland
* ✳ Aluminum foil

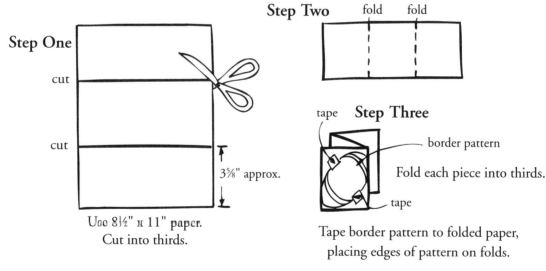

Step One

cut

cut

3⅝" approx.

Use 8½" x 11" paper.
Cut into thirds.

Step Two

fold   fold

Step Three

tape

border pattern

Fold each piece into thirds.

tape

Tape border pattern to folded paper,
placing edges of pattern on folds.

Step Four

Cut out pattern. Leave edges that touch folds uncut.

Borders will look
like this:

✻ Border Patterns ✻

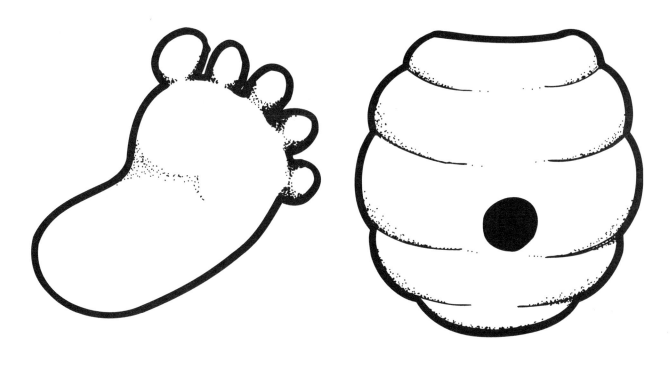

foot border

hive border

checkered border

leaf border

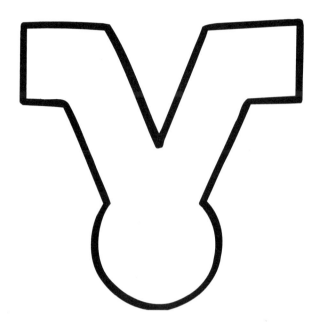

rick-rack border

trophy border

people border

shell border

✳ Border Patterns ✳

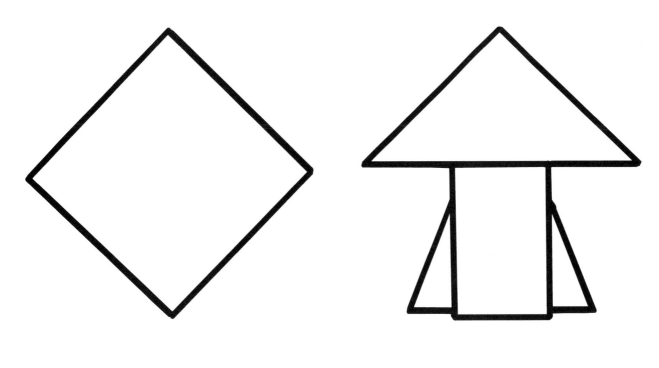

diamond border   rocket border

heart border   wave border

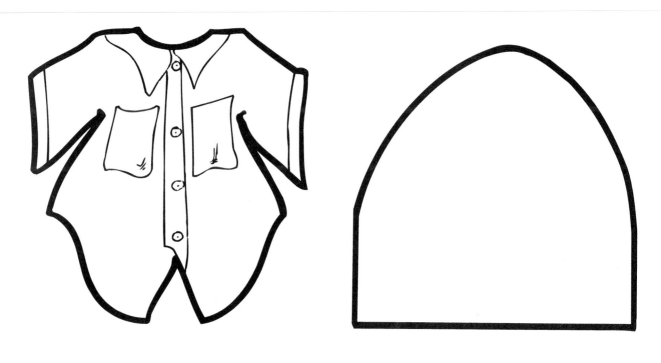

shirt border   semi-circle border

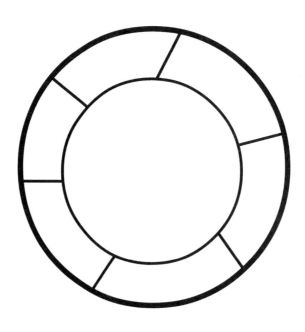

gem border

❋ Ages 2-5 ❋

❋ Plan

To identify religious freedom as an American value.

❋ Memorize

You will be free indeed. John 8:36

❋ Gather

- pattern for lettering from pp. 19-20
- pattern for checkered border from p. 11
- patterns for symbols of freedom from pp. 16-18
- poster board
- paper fasteners
- background paper, red
- crayons
- glue sticks

❋ Prepare

Duplicate the lettering on white construction paper. Duplicate the symbols of freedom on colored paper or on white paper and color with crayons or markers. Enlarge the symbols if needed. Cut two large circles from posterboard, also cutting a wedge from one as shown on the finished illustration above.

❋ Create

1. Attach the red background paper to the bulletin board. Cut out the lettering and post on the board as shown.
2. Cut and fold strips of blue construction paper according to the instant border directions on page 10. Trace the checkered border pattern onto the folded paper and cut out the border. Staple the border around the edges of the board.
3. Cut out the symbols of freedom and glue them to the dial without the cut-out wedge.
4. Attach the two dials together in the middle with a paper fastener, placing the wedge dial on top of the intact dial. Make sure that the wedge window shows the pictures when the dial is turned.
5. Attach the dials to the bulletin board by gently lifting the top dial and stapling only the bottom dial to the board so the top dial continues to move freely. Explain the symbols to the children as they turn the dial, then have them explain them to you.

❋ Teach

Make silhouettes of the children by attaching black construction paper to the wall and tracing each child's profile shadow on the paper with a white or silver crayon. The shadow will become more defined by placing a bright light beside the child. These silhouettes may then be attached to the bulletin board in a random fashion, and offered later as a take-home gift for parents.

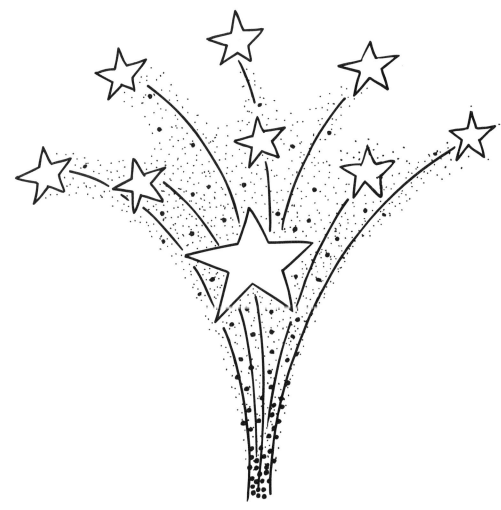

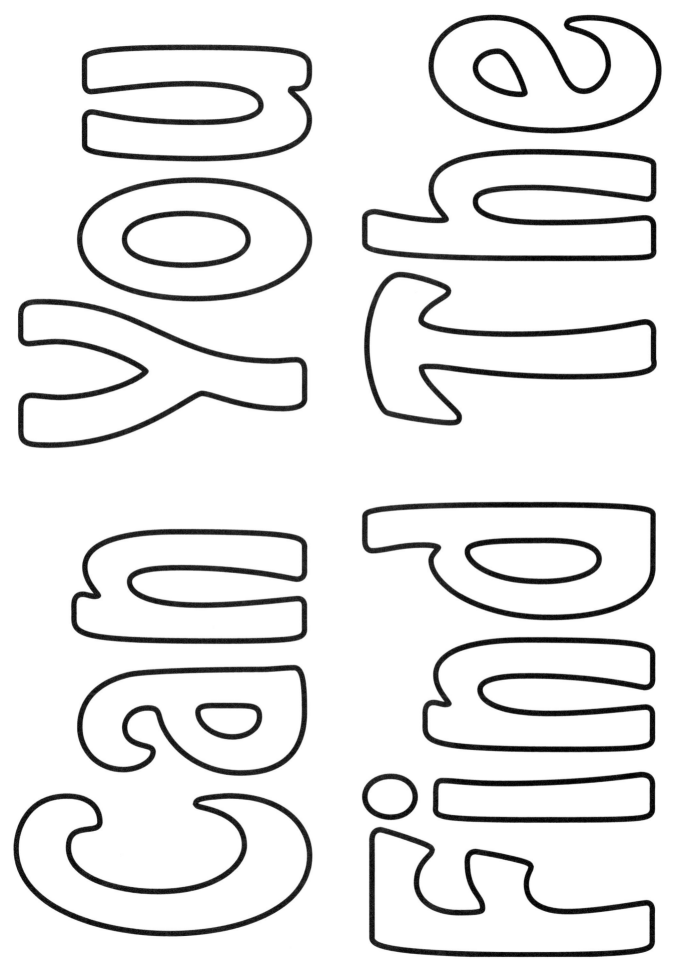

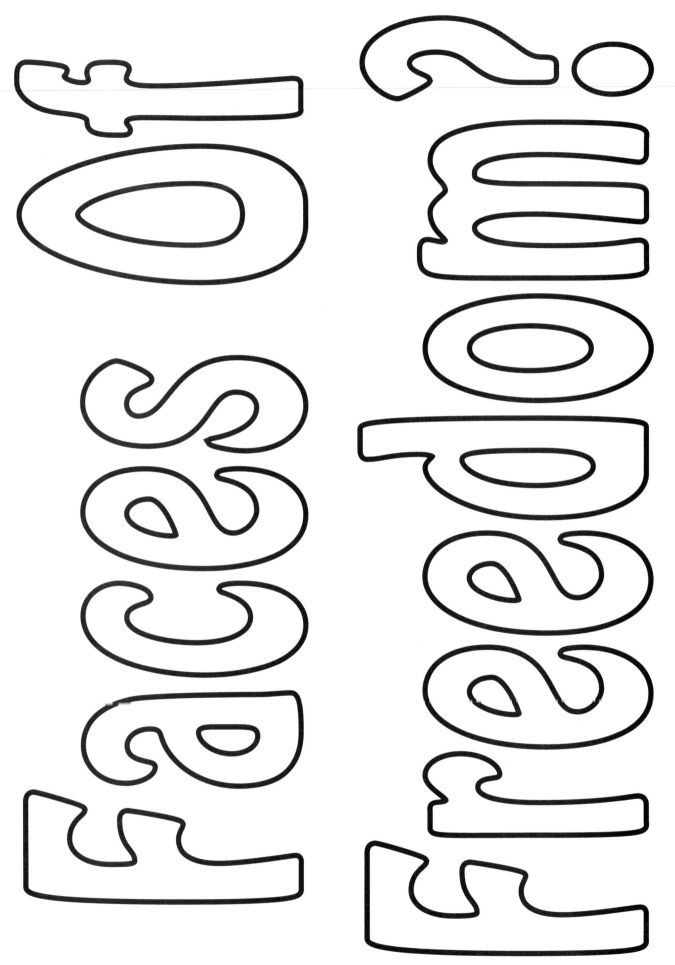

Faces of
Freedom!

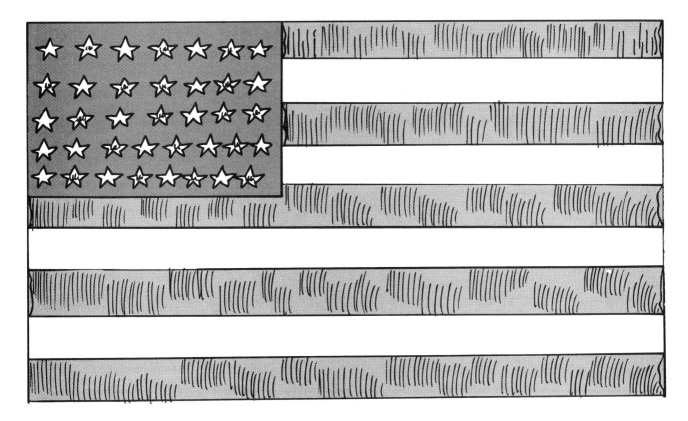

(Liberty)

✳ Plan
To celebrate the freedoms we have in America.

✳ Memorize
The truth will set you free. John 8:32

✳ Gather
• patterns for stars from p. 22
• background paper, white
• crepe paper streamers, red
• construction paper, blue and red
• construction paper stars, white
• marker, black
• glitter paint pens, silver

✳ Prepare
Duplicate the lettering on red construction paper. Duplicate 50 stars on white construction paper. There is no border around this bulletin board.

✳ Create
1. Attach the white background paper to the board.
2. Attach a blue construction paper rectangle at the top left corner of the board to hold the stars.
3. Stretch and staple the red crepe paper across the board to resemble the red stripes in the American flag, leaving white spaces between the red crepe stripes.
4. Cut out the stars. Set aside 8 stars on which to write one word of the memory verse and one each for the children in your class. Write each student's name on a star.
5. Distribute the remaining stars to the children and have them decorate them with the silver glitter paint pens. Attach the stars to the flag.

✳ Teach
Have a "Happy Birthday, America" party with your class. Bring red, white and blue gelatin squares or cupcakes decorated for the holiday. Sing patriotic songs. Bring miniature American flags for the students to wave as they march around the room. Say, **We should be thankful to God that we live in a place where we can say we love Him. Let's thank Him for that, and pray for the people in other countries where they cannot speak aloud about God.** Lead the class in a short prayer.

✳ Ages 6-10 ✳

✳ Plan
To understand that we are reflections of God to others.

✳ Memorize
Do everything without complaining or arguing, that you may become blameless and pure, children of God. Philippians 2:14-15

✳ Gather
• pattern for rocket from p. 24
• pattern for rocket border from p. 13
• pattern for lettering from p. 25
• background paper, black
• construction paper, red, white and blue
• chalk, white
• crayons
• glue
• glitter, silver or gold
• safety scissors

✳ Prepare
Duplicate the lettering on red, white and blue construction paper. Duplicate one rocket per child on white paper.

✳ Create
1. Cover the bulletin board with black background paper. Cut out the lettering and attach it to the board as shown. Use white chalk to write the memory verse on the board.

2. Cut and fold strips of red, white and blue construction paper according to the instant border directions on page 10. Trace the rocket border pattern onto the folded paper and cut out the border. Attach the border around the board's edges.

3. Distribute the rockets, crayons and scissors to the students. Have them color and cut out the rockets and put their names on them.

4. Attach the rockets to the bulletin board. Use glue and glitter to make fireworks—squiggly lines coming from each rocket!

✳ Teach
The memory verse related to this lesson is lengthy, so a game or activity may be helpful for the children to learn it. An easy one to try: Write the verse on the chalkboard. Erase one word at a time, reading what is left each time you erase the word. When the chalkboard is blank, do the game backwards by having the students call out words for the verse as you write them on the chalkboard.

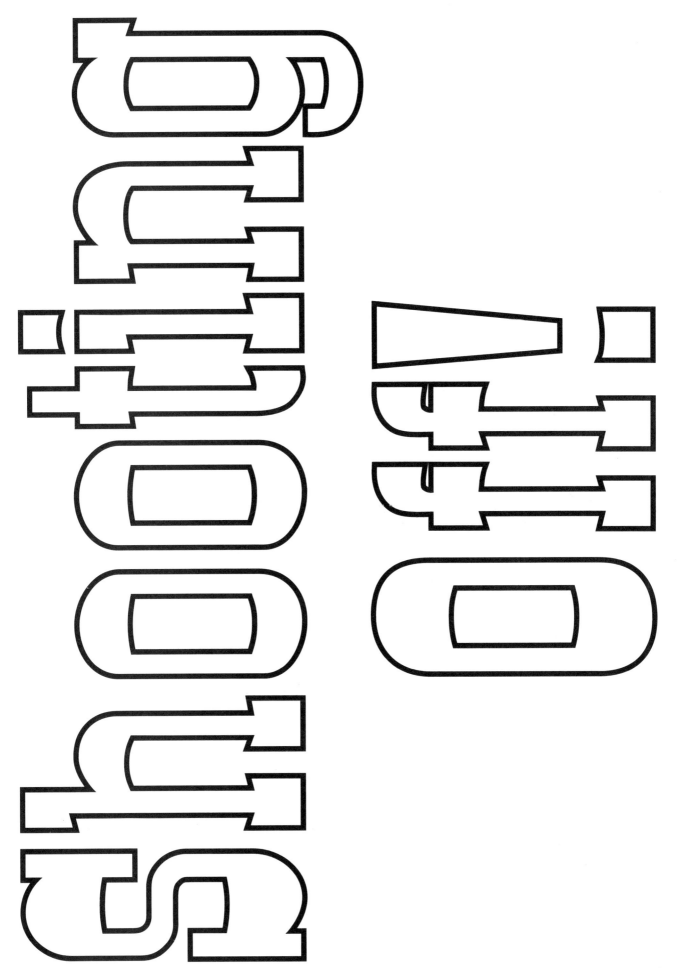

Shooting Star City Life

Fishing For Truth

✳ Ages 2-5 ✳

✳ Plan
To show that the Bible has answers for life.

✳ Memorize
I will make you fishers of men. Matthew 4:19

✳ Gather
- patterns for fisherman, fish and boat from pp. 27-29
- pattern for lettering from p. 30
- pattern for wave border from p. 13
- background paper, light and dark blue and brown
- construction paper, various
- yarn or string
- paper clip
- marker, black
- Velcro
- hole punch

✳ Prepare
Duplicate the lettering on yellow construction paper. Trace the boat half on a large folded piece of brown poster paper, cut out and unfold to make a large boat. Duplicate the fisherman on white paper. Duplicate the fish onto several colors of construction paper, two fish per color.

✳ Create
1. Attach the light blue background paper for the sky on the top half of the bulletin board and the dark blue background paper for the water on the bottom half of the bulletin board. Cut out the lettering and post as shown.
2. Cut and fold strips of blue construction paper according to the instant border directions on page 10. Trace the wave border pattern onto the folded paper and cut out

the border. Staple the border around the edges of the board.
3. Attach the boat to the board, sitting on the water. Make extra waves using the dark blue paper and the wave border pattern, then attach them along the side of the boat. Gently bend the waves away from the board to enhance your bulletin board.
4. Cut out the fisherman and color or glue pieces of fabric on him for clothing. Place him "in" the boat and secure.
5. Cut a length of yarn and tie a straightened paper clip to one end of it. Attach the other end of yarn to the fishing pole.
6. Cut out the fish. Arrange and attach one of each color to the bulletin board in the water. On the other fish, write a scripture on the front, attach a piece of Velcro to its back and punch a hole near the mouth of the fish.
7. Attach the corresponding piece of Velcro to the fish on the bulletin board. The children may match the fish on the bulletin board to the same color of fish they hold. Besides encouraging color recognition, the fish may be moved around the board and placed on the hook.

✳ Teach
You may use this bulletin as a long-term memory verse aid. Look ahead in your curriculum and use the memory verses for coming weeks on the fish. Encourage the children to learn the scripture that you place on the fisherman's hook each week. Help the children to "read" and understand each verse. Say, **God helped people to write the Bible so we could live better. You can always find the right answers in the Bible.**

Place on fold and cut on solid lines

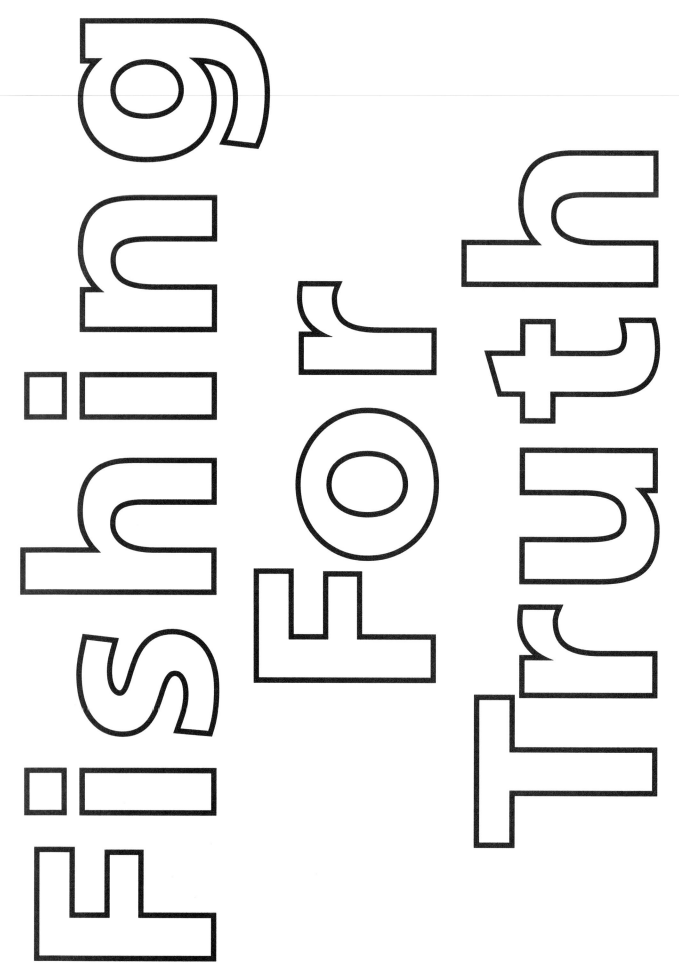

＊ Plan

To understand the importance of knowing the Bible.

＊ Memorize

I have hidden your word in my heart. Psalm 119:11

＊ Gather

- pattern for fish, Bible and story illustrations from pp. 32-35
- pattern for lettering from pp. 36-37
- pattern for wave border from p. 13
- background paper, blue
- construction paper, green and black
- yarn or string
- paper clips
- stapler
- tape
- hole punch
- glue sticks

＊ Prepare

Duplicate the lettering on yellow construction paper and the fish pattern on various colors of paper. Duplicate the Bible pattern and the story pictures on white paper, one set per child.

＊ Create

1. Cover the bulletin board with the blue paper. Cut out the lettering and attach it to the board as shown.
2. Cut and fold strips of blue construction paper according to the instant border directions on page 10. Trace the wave border pattern onto the folded paper and cut out the border. Staple the border around the edges of the board.
3. Attach one piece of yarn per student to the top of the board as shown.
4. Bend paper clips to look like hooks and tie one to each length of yarn.
5. Cut out the fish and attach them randomly on the board.
6. Fold the Bibles in half so "Holy Bible" is on the front. Write the student's name on the back of each Bible. Use the hole punch to make a hole in the top left-hand corner of each booklet.
7. Fold and staple the Bible story pages inside the covers (place back-to-back). Cover staples with tape to avoid injury.
8. Distribute the Bibles and crayons to the children.
9. Hang the Bibles on the paper clips. The children may open their "Bibles," take them off the hook and put them back.

＊ Teach

Make a "Bible" booklet (use the Bible pattern page again) for each child and write his or her name on the front right-hand corner. As the children learn to recite the books of the Bible in order give them a sticker for their booklet.

HOLY BIBLE

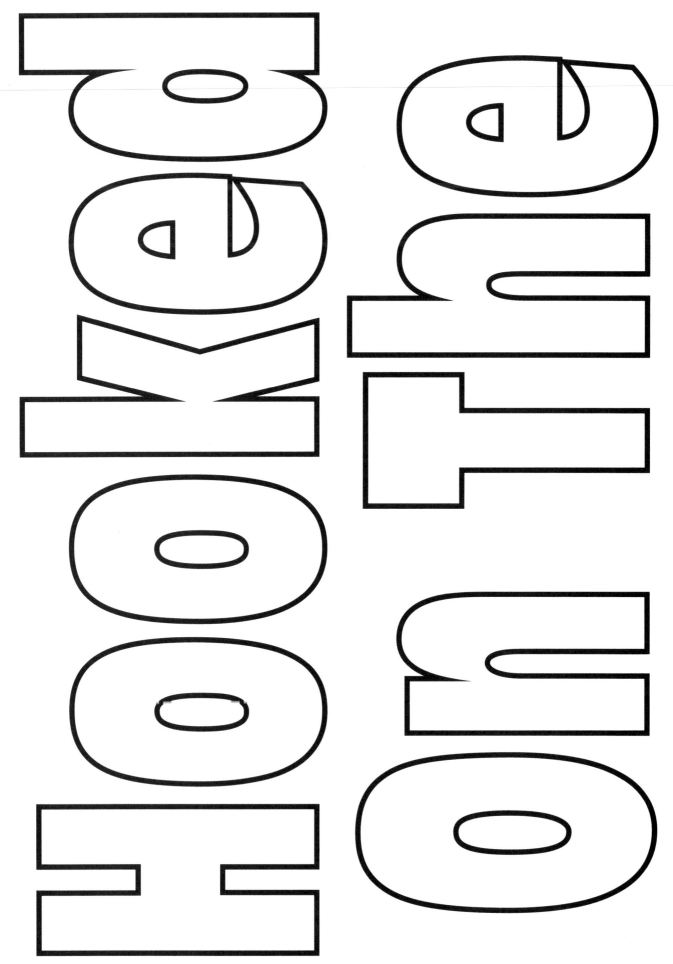

❋ Ages 2-5 ❋

❋ Plan
To learn to give Jesus control for everything.

❋ Memorize
Commit to the Lord whatever you do.
Proverbs 16:3

❋ Gather
- pattern for lettering from pp. 41-42
- pattern for diamond border from p. 13
- pattern for flags, circle and golf ball from pp. 39-40
- background paper, blue
- felt, green
- construction paper, various colors
- sandpaper scraps
- glue
- plastic drinking straws

❋ Prepare
Duplicate the lettering on white construction paper and four triangle flags on various colors of paper. Duplicate four circles on black construction paper. Duplicate the golf ball on white paper, one per child.

❋ Create
1. Attach the blue background paper to the board for the sky and the green felt for grass. Cut out the lettering and post it as shown.
2. Cut and fold strips of white construction paper according to the instant border directions on page 10. Trace the diamond border pattern onto the folded paper and cut out the border. Staple the border around the board's edges.
3. Cut out the triangle flags and write the numbers 1 through 4 on them.
4. Cut out the black circles and make a slit in the center of each.
5. Flatten one end each of four straws and slip them in the slits of the black circles. Attach the circles and straws to the board on the green felt.
6. Staple a flag to each straw.
7. Cut out the golf balls. Write each child's name on the front of one and glue a small piece of sandpaper to the back.
8. Every week the child is present he or she may move the golf ball to a flag with a higher number. For example, if the child is present two weeks then his or her ball is placed near the hole with flag number two.

❋ Teach
Explain the term "hole-in-one" to the students so they understand its significance. Reward them for their "golf" efforts with a party at a miniature golf course. Bring small prizes for those who achieve pre-set goals, like shortest or longest putt.

38

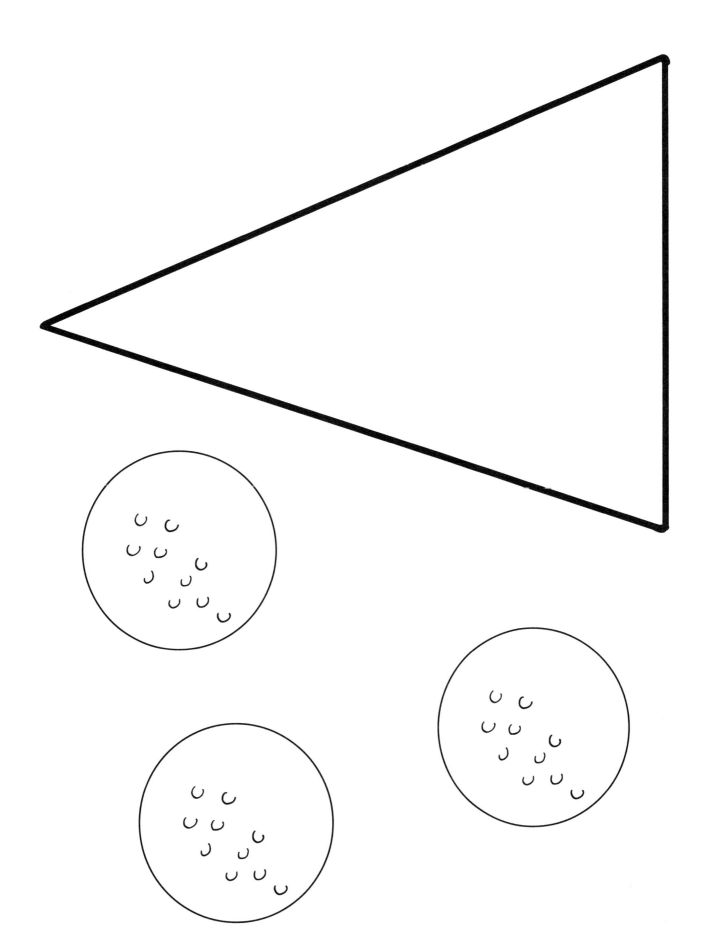

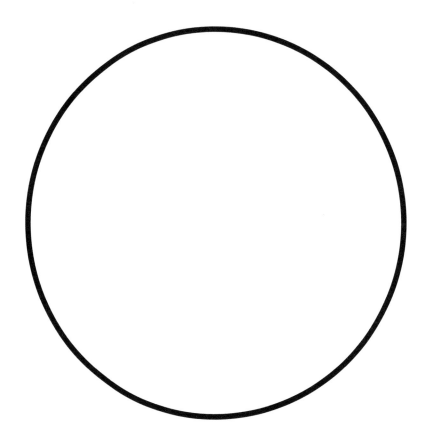

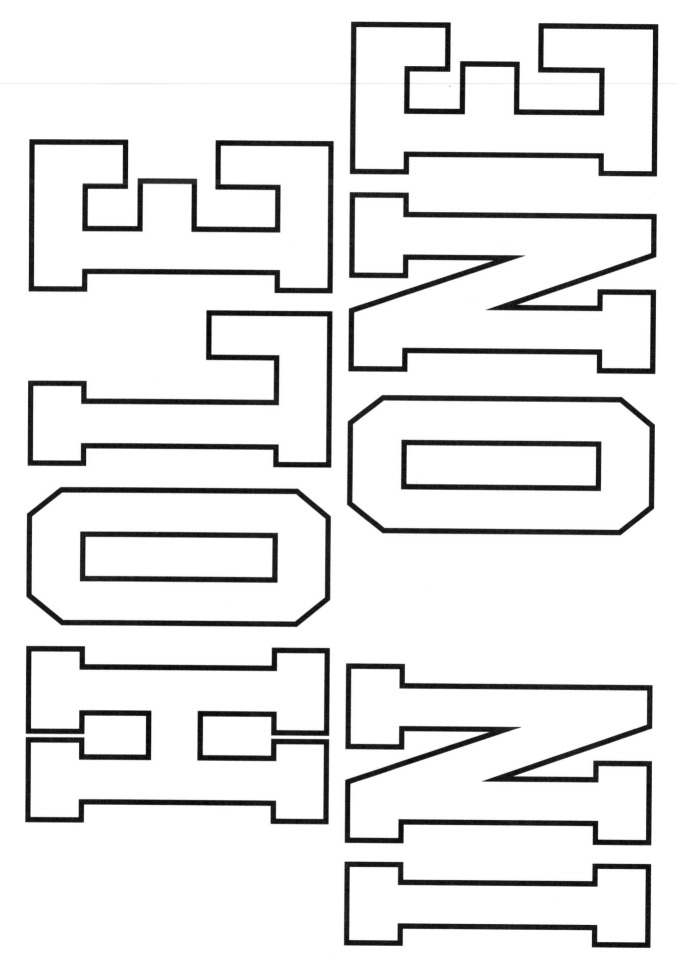

Pleasant words are a honeycomb, sweet to the soul and healing to the bones. Proverbs 16:24

✳ Ages 6-10 ✳

✳ Plan
To emphasize the importance of kind words.

✳ Memorize
Pleasant words are a honeycomb, sweet to the soul and healing to the bones. Proverbs 16:24

✳ Gather
- patterns for bee from p. 44
- pattern for hive border from p. 11
- pattern for lettering from p. 45
- background paper, blue
- construction paper, black and brown
- poster paper, brown
- marker, black
- crayons
- safety scissors

✳ Prepare
Duplicate the lettering on black paper. Draw a large bee hive (see illustration above) on brown poster paper. Duplicate a bee for each student on white paper.

✳ Create
1. Cover the bulletin board with blue background paper. Cut out the lettering and the bee hive. Attach the lettering and the hive to the bulletin board as shown. Use a black marker to write the Bible verse at the bottom of the board.
2. Cut and fold strips of brown construction paper according to the instant border directions on page 10. Trace the hive border pattern onto the folded paper and cut out the border. Attach the border around the board's edges.
3. Distribute the bees to the students. Have them color and cut out the bees, then write on their bees a polite word or phrase ("please," "thank you," "you're welcome," etc.).
4. Attach the bees to the board.

✳ Teach
Ask, **Why is it important to be polite to other people? Why is it especially important for Christians to be polite to others? How can we practice being polite?** Have the children turn to each of their neighbors and say something polite.

Daisy Prayer Chain

Pray continually; give thanks in all circumstances, for this is God's will for you in Christ Jesus.
1 Thessalonians 5:17-18

* Ages 6-10 *

* Plan
To learn about prayer requests and answers.

* Memorize
Pray continually; give thanks in all circumstances, for this is God's will for you in Christ Jesus.
1 Thessalonians 5:17-18

* Gather
- pattern for lettering from p. 48
- pattern for daisy parts from p. 47
- pattern for leaf border from p. 11
- background paper, blue
- construction paper, green, yellow and orange
- marker, black
- pencils
- glue
- safety scissors

* Prepare
Duplicate the lettering on green construction paper. Duplicate the daisy patterns on white paper, one set for each child.

* Create
1. Cover the bulletin board with blue background paper. Cut out the lettering and attach it to the board as shown. Use a black marker to write the Bible verse on the bottom of the board.

2. Cut and fold strips of green construction paper according to the instant border directions on p. 10. Trace the leaf border pattern onto the folded paper and cut out the border. Attach the border around the board's edges.

3. Distribute the daisy patterns and construction paper to the students. Have the students trace and cut the center of the daisy from yellow or orange construction paper, the petals from white construction paper and the leaf from green construction paper. Show how to assemble the daisy and glue it together. Ask the students to write a prayer request in the center of their daisies.

4. Attach the daisies to the board.

* Teach
After the daisies have been displayed, lead a class prayer and mention every student's prayer request in your prayer. Each week that the board is displayed, ask the students if they feel that God has answered their requests. If a student affirms that he or she did receive an answer to prayer, have the students write "Answered!" on a leaf and attach it to the corresponding daisy.

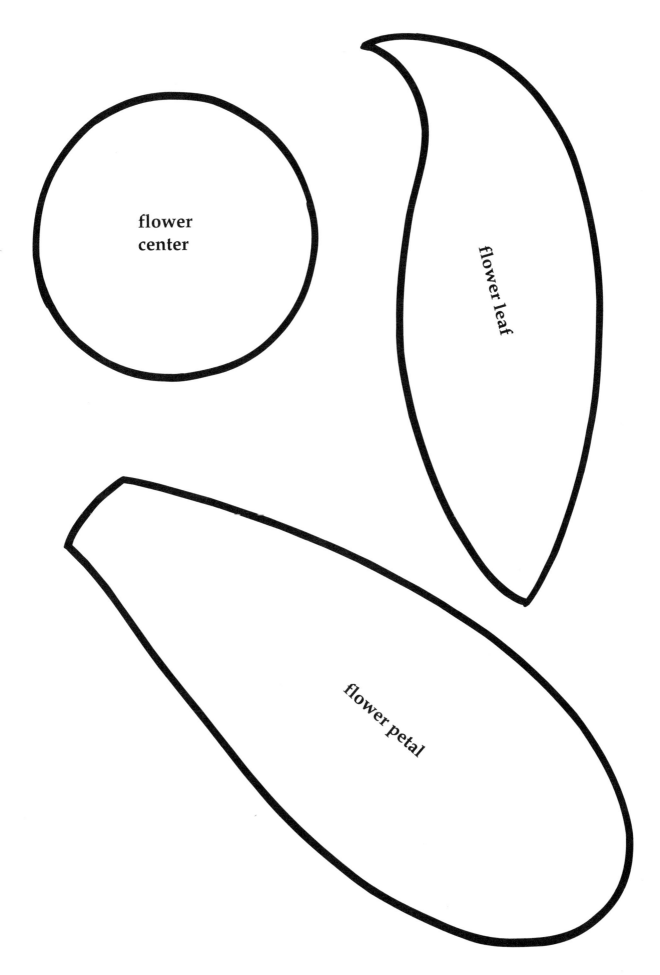

flower center

flower leaf

flower petal

Daisy

Prayer

Chain

* Plan

To understand that we are to be an example of God's love.

* Memorize

Bear[ing] fruit in every good work. Colossians 1:10

* Gather

• patterns for watermelon from pp. 50-51
• pattern for lettering from p. 52
• pattern for checkered border from p. 11
• background paper, yellow
• construction paper, green and red
• glue
• marker, black
• watermelon seeds

* Prepare

Duplicate the lettering on red construction paper. Duplicate the watermelon patterns on red and green construction paper as indicated on the patterns.

* Create

1. Attach the yellow background paper to the bulletin board. Cut out the lettering and post it on the board as shown.
2. Cut and fold strips of red construction paper according to the instant border directions on page 10. Trace the checkered border pattern onto the folded paper and cut out the border. Staple the border around the edges of the board.
3. Cut out the watermelon patterns and glue them together as shown.
4. Write a child's name on the rind of each watermelon.
5. Attach the watermelons to the bulletin boards.
6. Have the children glue a watermelon seed each day they are present, bring their Bibles, repeat a memory verse or whatever act you deem appropriate.

* Teach

Explain the concept of "fruitful lives" to the children. Say, **God gives us good fruit to eat, like watermelon, apples and oranges. Why do we like to eat fruit? God also likes for us to "be fruit." Does that mean we should all look like watermelons? No! That means God wants us to be good people. We should show His love by being sweet like fruit. Then other people will want to be like us and follow God.**

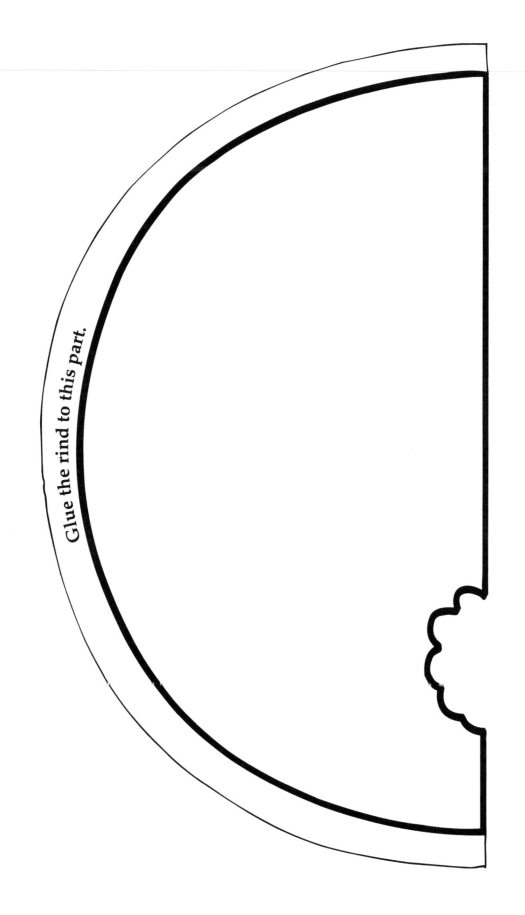

Glue the rind to this part.

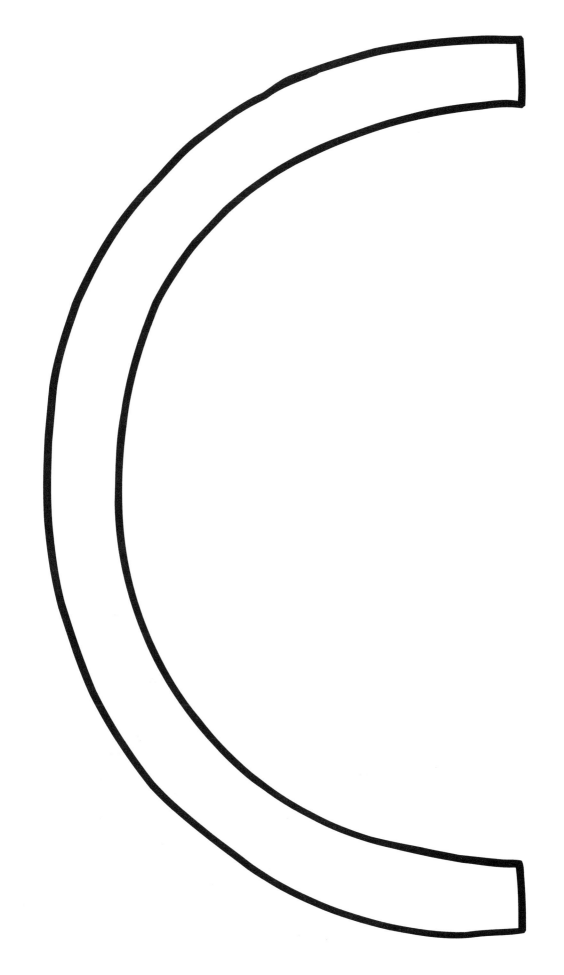

51

* Plan

To emphasize that God is the giver of nature.

* Memorize

The rain and the snow come down from heaven.
Isaiah 55:10

* Gather

- pattern for lettering from p. 58
- pattern for diamond border from p. 13
- patterns for watering can, flower pot and flower from pp. 54-57
- background paper, yellow
- construction paper, brown, gray and various colors
- glue stick
- marker, black

* Prepare

Duplicate the lettering on black construction paper, and the watering can parts on gray paper. Duplicate the flower pot on brown construction paper, one per child. Duplicate five flower petals, two leaves and one flower center on various colors of paper, one set per child. Cut stems freehand from green paper.

* Create

1. Attach the yellow background paper to the bulletin board. Cut out the lettering and post it as shown.
2. Cut and fold strips of black construction paper according to the instant border directions on page 10. Trace the diamond border pattern onto the folded paper and cut out the border. Staple the border around the edges of the board.
3. Cut out the watering can and flower pots and attach them to the bulletin board as shown, leaving the top of each flower pot open like a pocket for the children's flowers.
4. Cut out the flower petals, centers and leaves for each flower.
5. Have the children put their flowers together using the glue sticks.
6. Write the children's names on the center of each flower with a black marker. Also write virtues that are taught in your class on each flower petal (sharing, kindness, loving, etc.).
7. When the flowers are completed, have the children slide their flowers into their flower pots on the bulletin board.

* Teach

Ask, **Does anyone know why God makes it rain? God gives us everything we need to live. He gives us rain and sunshine to make our plants grow. He gives us food to eat. He gives us each other so we can talk and play. Let's make God happy by thanking Him for all of the things He gives us.** Lead in a short prayer of thanks.

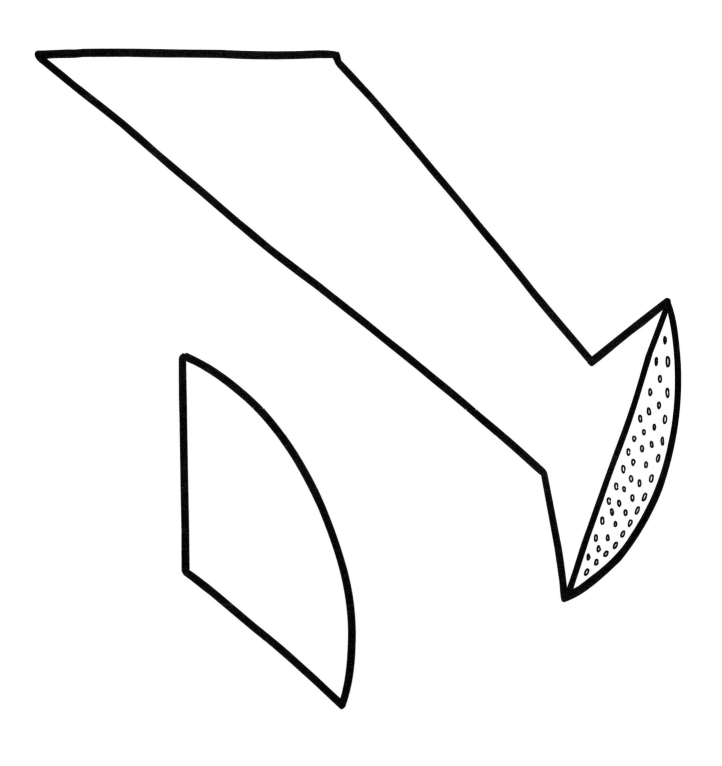

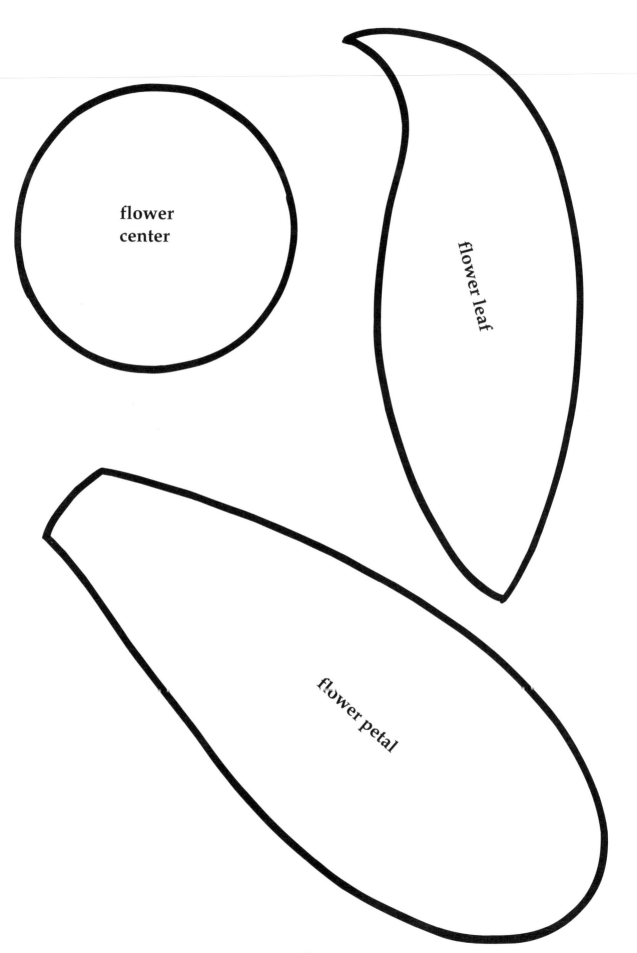

flower center

flower leaf

flower petal

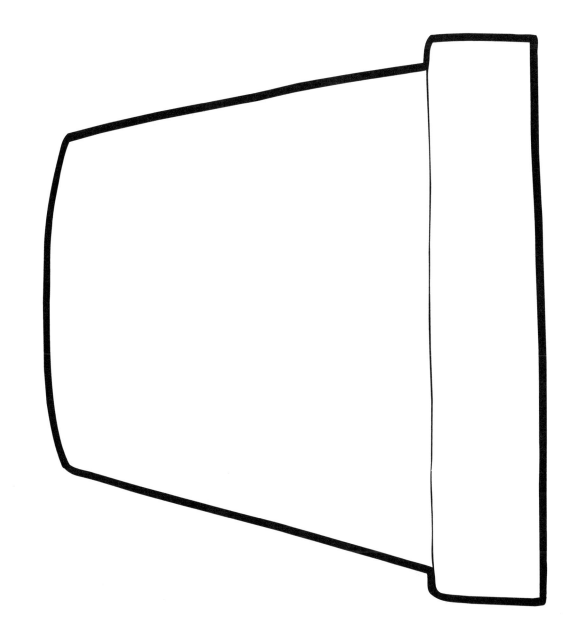

In All

Growing

Good Ways

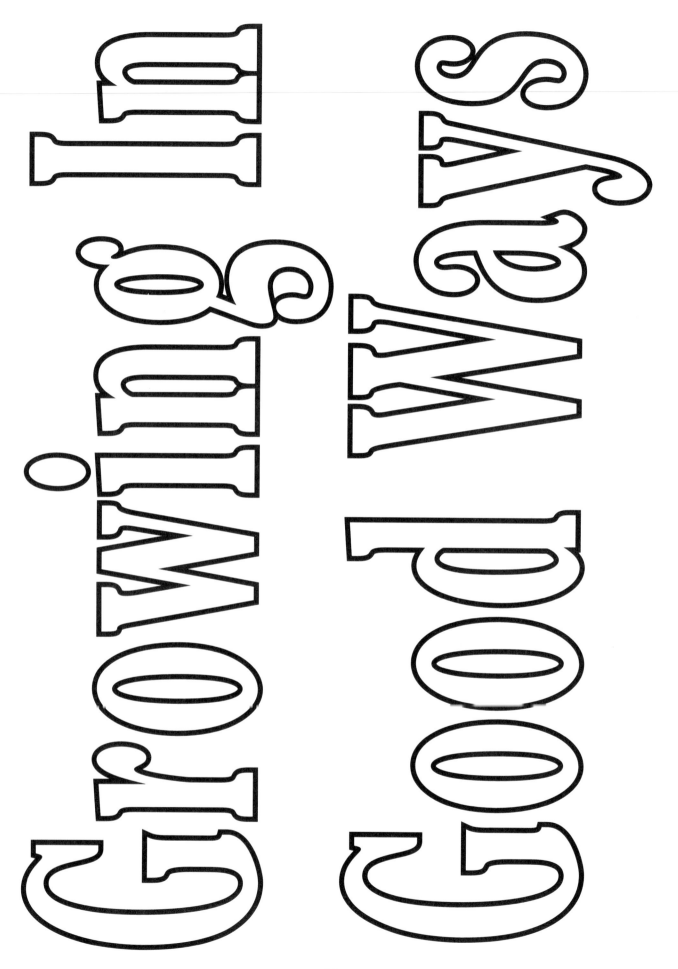

Walk in the light, as he is in the light. 1 John 1:7

✳ Ages 6-10 ✳

✳ Plan
To learn that Jesus is the Light of the world.

✳ Memorize
Walk in the light, as he is in the light. 1 John 1:7

✳ Gather
- pattern for sunglasses from p. 60
- pattern for rick-rack border from p. 12
- pattern for lettering from pp. 61-62
- background paper, bright blue
- construction paper or poster paper, yellow
- paper, white
- chalk, yellow
- marker, black
- safety scissors
- construction paper, assorted scraps
- glitter, feathers, beads
- plastic wrap, colored
- glue

✳ Prepare
Duplicate the lettering on yellow construction paper. Duplicate the sunglasses pattern on white paper, one per child.

✳ Create
1. Cover the bulletin board with bright blue background paper. Cut a large circle wedge from yellow construction paper or poster paper to fit in the board's upper left corner. Draw rays with yellow chalk.

2. Cut out the lettering and attach it to the board as shown. Use a black marker to write the Bible verse at the bottom of the board.

3. Cut and fold strips of yellow construction paper according to the instant border directions on page 10. Trace the rickrack border pattern onto the folded paper and cut out the border. Attach the border around the board's edges.

4. Distribute the sunglasses to the student. Have the students cut out the pattern and use it to trace and cut glasses from colorful construction paper. Allow the students to decorate their glasses with beads, glitter, feathers and paper scraps. Make "lenses" by gluing colored plastic wrap to the back of each lens opening.

5. Attach the completed glasses to the bulletin board.

✳ Teach
Ask, **What is a Son?** The children will probably assume you mean the sun in the sky or a male child. **What if I make the s a capital S? Which Son are we talking about then? What does it mean when we want the Son—S-O-N— to shine? Can we help Him to shine? Let's try to walk with Jesus. He will light our paths.**

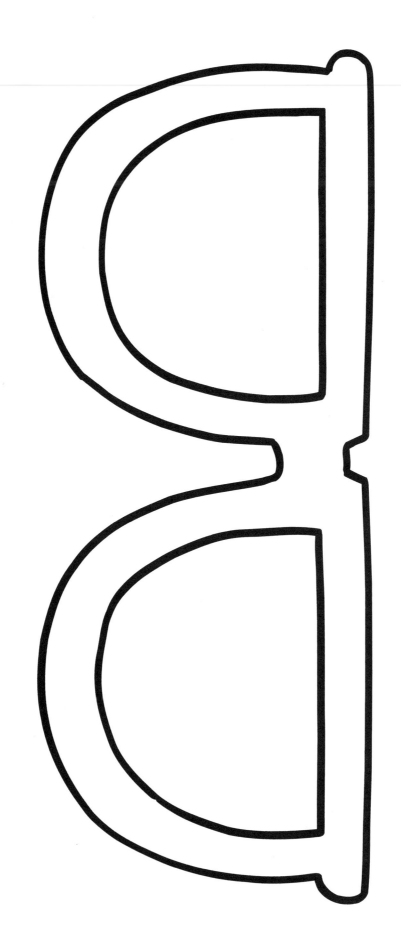

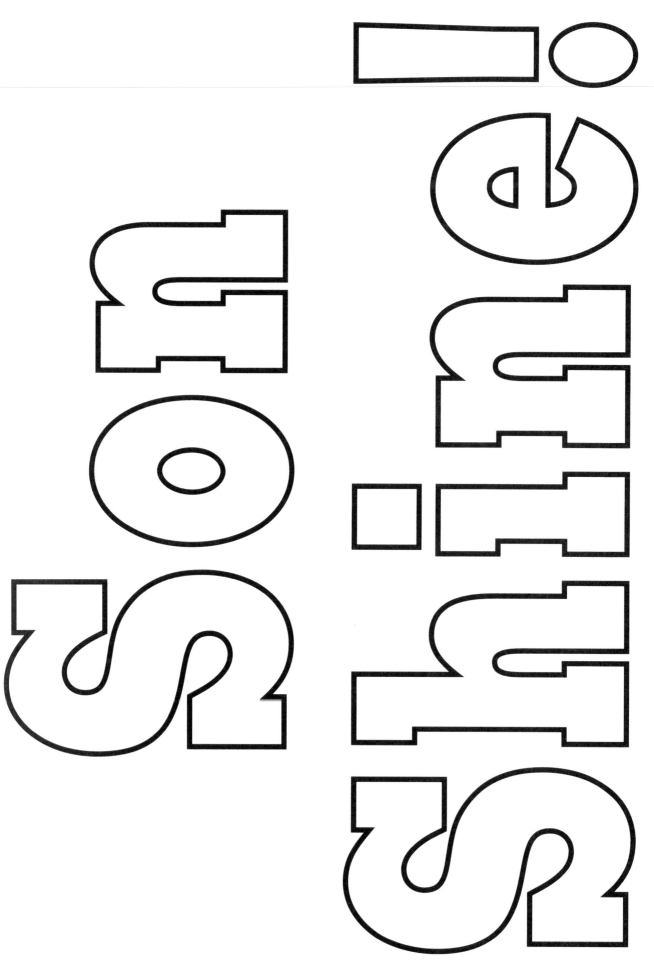

62

* Ages 2-5 *

* Plan

To understand that God nourishes our spirits.

* Memorize

I will provide for you there. Genesis 45:11

* Gather

- patterns for Bible, praying hands, church and flatware from pp. 64-65
- pattern for lettering from p. 66
- pattern for checkered border from p. 11
- background paper, red
- construction paper, black and white
- paper plates, 9" size
- paper cups
- napkins
- crayons
- glue sticks
- Velcro
- marker, black

* Prepare

Duplicate the lettering and flatware on black construction paper, one set of flatware per student. Duplicate the Bible, praying hands and church on white paper, making enough that each child may select one.

* Create

1. Attach the red background paper to the board, or use a red and white checked paper tablecloth. Cut out the lettering and post it as shown.

2. Cut and fold strips of black construction paper according to the instant border directions on page 10. Trace the checkered border pattern onto the folded paper and cut out the border. Staple the border around the board's edges.

3. Cut out the flatware, Bibles, praying hands and churches. Have each child select and color one of the latter three and glue it to the center of a paper plate.

4. Write each child's name on a cup with a black marker and place a small piece of Velcro on the backs of the cups and plates. Attach the corresponding pieces of Velcro to the bulletin board in place setting arrangements. Post these pieces and staple on a napkin and flatware as shown above. The children may remove and replace their cups and plates from the bulletin board.

* Teach

Serve a nutritious snack, such as raisins and pretzels. Then discuss with the children how these foods nourish your body, and how the things on the bulletin board will nourish our spirits and make us feel better.

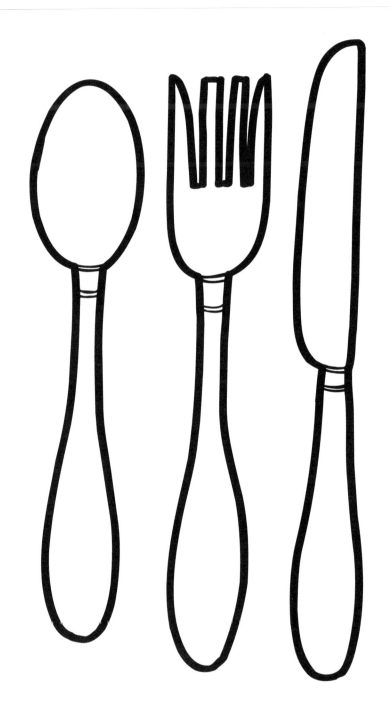

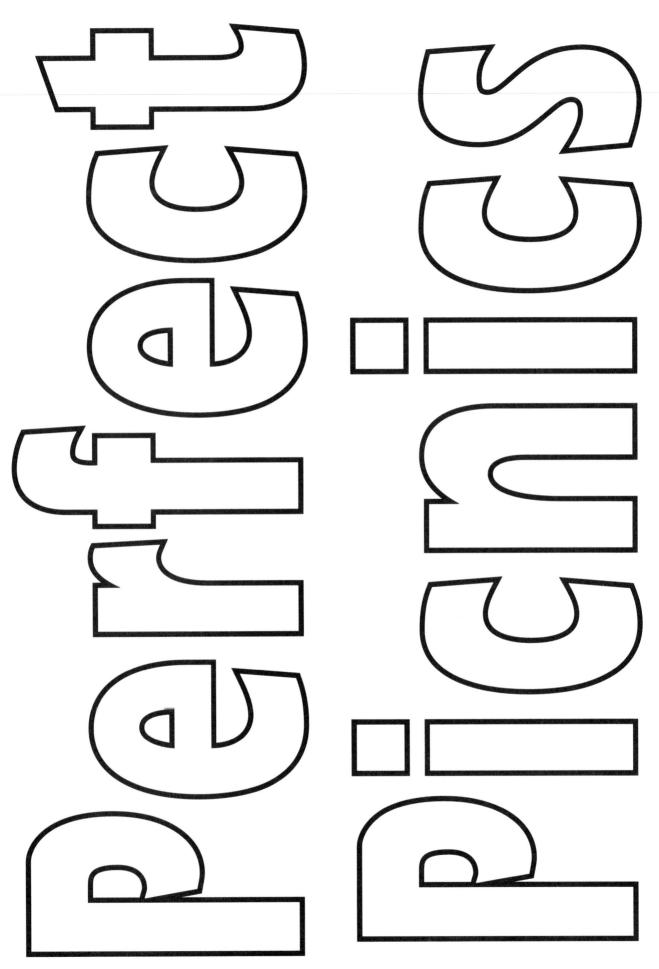

Perfect Picnics

✳ Ages 2-5 ✳

✳ Plan
To understand that God is the Creator of everything.

✳ Memorize
The Lord will be our Mighty One. Isaiah 33:21

✳ Gather
- pattern for lettering from pp. 70-71
- pattern for boat and sail from pp. 68-69
- pattern for wave border from p. 13
- background, light and dark blue
- white polyfil
- poster paper, various colors
- plastic drinking straws
- construction paper, orange
- magazines
- safety scissors
- glue sticks

✳ Prepare
Duplicate the lettering on orange construction paper. Trace the sail and boat on contrasting colors of poster paper that are folded in half. Cut them away from the fold so they open into larger sails and boats. Make one sail and one boat per child.

✳ Create
1. Attach the light blue background paper to the top half of the bulletin board and the dark blue paper to the bottom half of the board. For a three-dimensional effect, add two different sizes and layers of waves. Bend the waves away from the board.

2. Cut and fold strips of orange construction paper according to the instant border directions on page 10. Trace the wave border pattern onto the folded paper and cut out the border. Staple the border around the board's edges.

3. Glue the polyfil in the sky for clouds.

4. Cut out the boats and sails. Unfold the boat, write each child's name on one and attach it to the bulletin board.

5. Open the sail and staple it along the fold and on the bulletin board. The sail should flap open.

6. Attach the straw mast to the bulletin board by securing it slightly under the sail fold.

7. Attach the bottom of the boat to the straw mast.

8. Have the children look for pictures in magazines that are the same color as the sails on their boats. They may cut them out and glue them to the inside of the sail on the bulletin board.

✳ Teach
Discuss the pictures that the children chose. Ask whether God made the item or humans made it (for example: green grass or a green car). Say, **Some of the things we have were created by God, like nature. Some things are made by people like you and me who use the brain that God gave them to make it. Either way, God is the Creator of everything and we should praise Him for all that He gives us.**

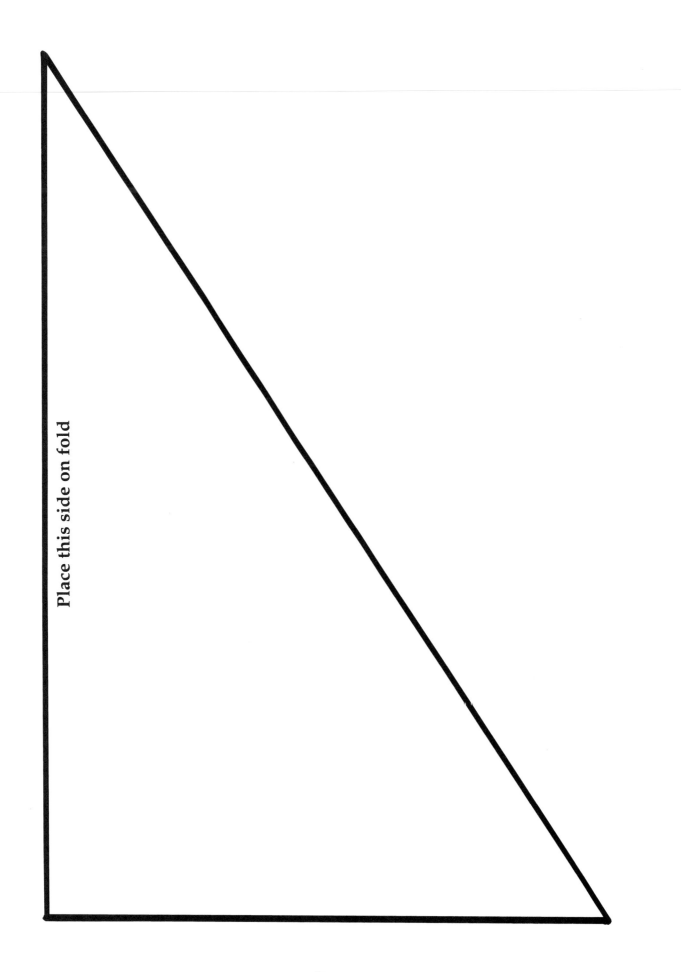

Place this side on fold

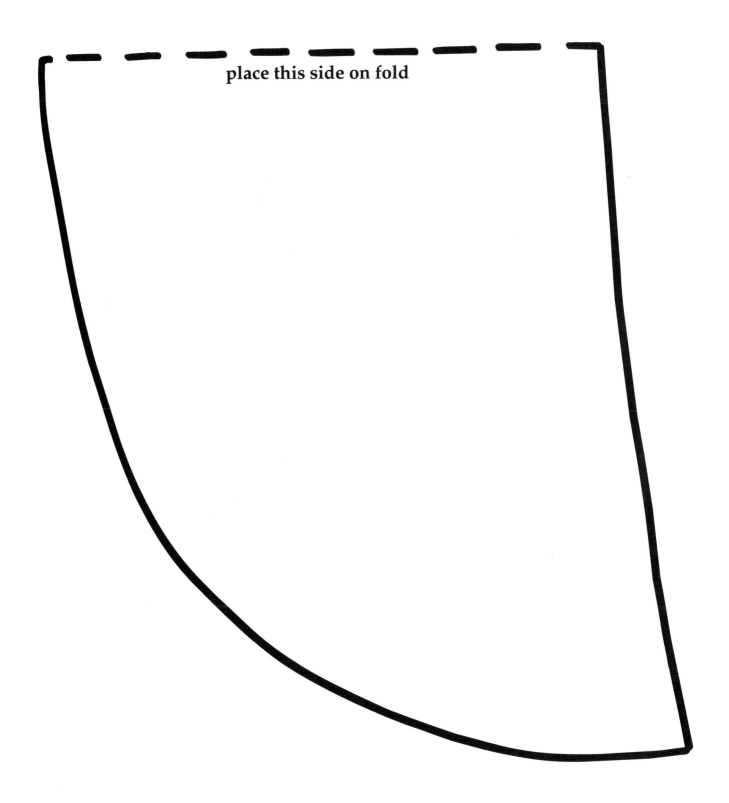

place this side on fold

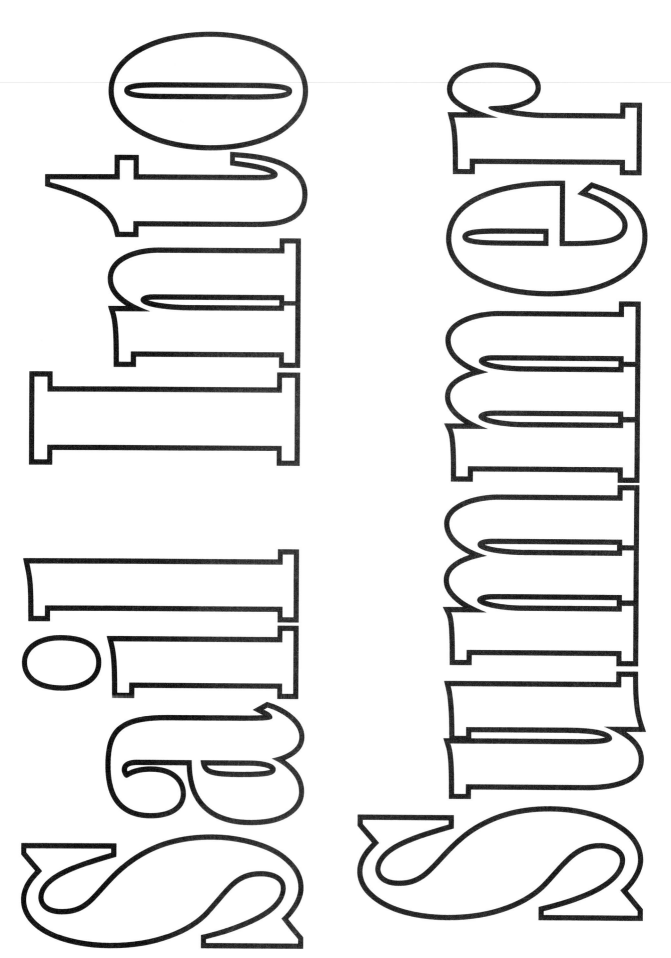

Sail Into Summer

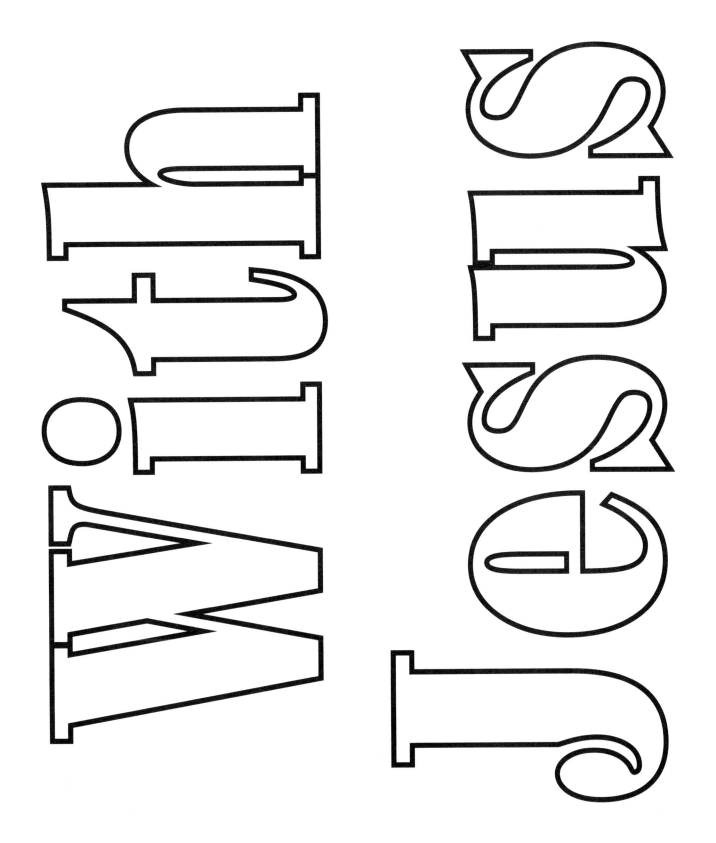

✳ **Ages 6-10** ✳

✳ **Plan**

To learn that we are to enjoy God.

✳ **Memorize**

Select a verse from those on page 73.

✳ **Gather**

- pattern for bucket and shovel from pp. 73-74
- pattern for shell border from p. 12
- pattern for lettering from p. 75
- poster paper, light brown
- marker, black
- construction paper, blue, gray, white and assorted
- push pin
- plastic sandwich bag

✳ **Prepare**

Duplicate the lettering on blue construction paper. Duplicate 10 buckets on brightly-colored construction paper and 10 shovels on gray construction paper.

✳ **Create**

1. Cover the bulletin board with light brown poster paper. Cut out the lettering and attach it to the board as shown.
2. Cut and fold strips of white construction paper according to the instant border directions on page 10. Trace the shell border pattern onto the folded paper and cut out the border. Staple the border around the board's edges.
3. Cut out the buckets and shovels. On each bucket, use a black marker to write one of the numbered Bible verses from page 73.
4. Write the corresponding reference from p. 73 on the front of each shovel and the correct number answer on the back. Cover the shovels and buckets with clear, self-stick plastic. Store them in a plastic sandwich bag attached with a push pin to the lower right corner of the board.
5. Attach the buckets to the board, leaving the tops open. Challenge the students to match the Bible references with the correct verses. They may check their work by turning the shovels over.

✳ **Teach**

Read Jesus' teaching about the wise and foolish builders from Matthew 7:24-27 to the children. To illustrate the story, have on hand rocks, sand, water and a toy house. Demonstrate how the house on sand is swept away by the water but the house on rocks remains. Explain that we should build our lives on the Rock, Jesus, if we want to live eternally.

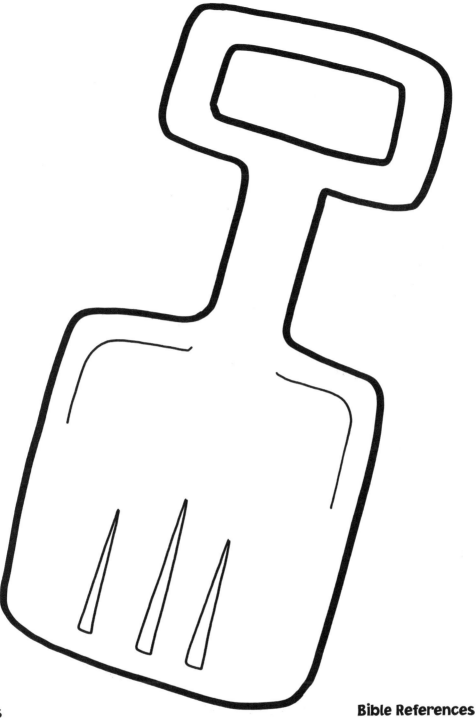

Bible Verses

1. This is how we know what love is: Jesus Christ laid down his life for us.
2. I have loved you with an everlasting love.
3. Cast all your anxiety on him because he cares for you.
4. My God will meet all your needs according to his glorious riches in Christ Jesus.
5. Do not let your hearts be troubled and do not be afraid.
6. He will command his angels concerning you to guard you in all your ways.
7. The Lord will keep you from all harm—he will watch over your life.
8. I can do everything through him who gives me strength.
9. I praise you because I am fearfully and wonderfully made.
10. All the days ordained for me were written in your book before one of them came to be.

Bible References

1. 1 John 3:16
2. Jeremiah 31:3
3. 1 Peter 5:7
4. Philippians 4:19
5. John 14:27
6. Psalm 91:11
7. Psalm 121:7
8. Philippians 4:13
9. Psalm 139:14
10. Psalm 139:16

Sand And

Scripture

✳ Ages 6-10 ✳

✳ Plan
To learn about numbers in the Bible.

✳ Memorize
He determines the number of the stars and calls them each by name. Psalm 147:4

✳ Gather
• pattern for lettering from p. 79
• pattern for ladybug from pp. 77-78
• pattern for semi-circle border from p. 14
• background paper, white
• construction paper, black and red
• marker, black
• paper fasteners
• hole punch
• glue
• index cards, white 3" × 5"

✳ Prepare
Duplicate the lettering and 10 ladybug bodies on black construction paper. Duplicate 10 of each ladybug wing on red construction paper.

✳ Create
1. Cover the bulletin board with the white background paper. Cut out the lettering and attach it to the board as shown. Use a black marker to write the Bible verse on the board.
2. Cut and fold strips of black construction paper according to the instant border directions on page 10. Trace the semi-circle border pattern onto the folded paper and cut out the border. Attach the border around the board's edges.
3. Cut out the ladybug bodies and wings. Assemble the ladybugs by laying the wings on top of the body and punching holes in the wings and the bodies. Place a paper fastener through the hole, connecting the wings together to make a shell.
4. Cut circles from black construction paper and glue the spots onto the outside of the shells. Open the wings and glue an index card on each ladybug body. Attach the ladybugs to the bulletin board, leaving space between them for writing.
5. Below each ladybug, use a black marker to write one of the "number" questions from page 77. The answers in parentheses should be copied onto the corresponding ladybug's index card.
6. Call the students' attention to the bulletin board. Invite them to discover more about numbers by reading the question below each ladybug and writing down the answers on scrap paper. They may check their answers by opening the wings of each ladybug.

✳ Teach
Show your students how to use a Bible concordance — or allow them to work from memory — and challenge them to devise their own lists of number questions. Then have the class pair off and share their questions with one another or have each child select a question to read to the class. Or, play "Stump the Teacher" and have the kids try to outsmart you with their clever questions.

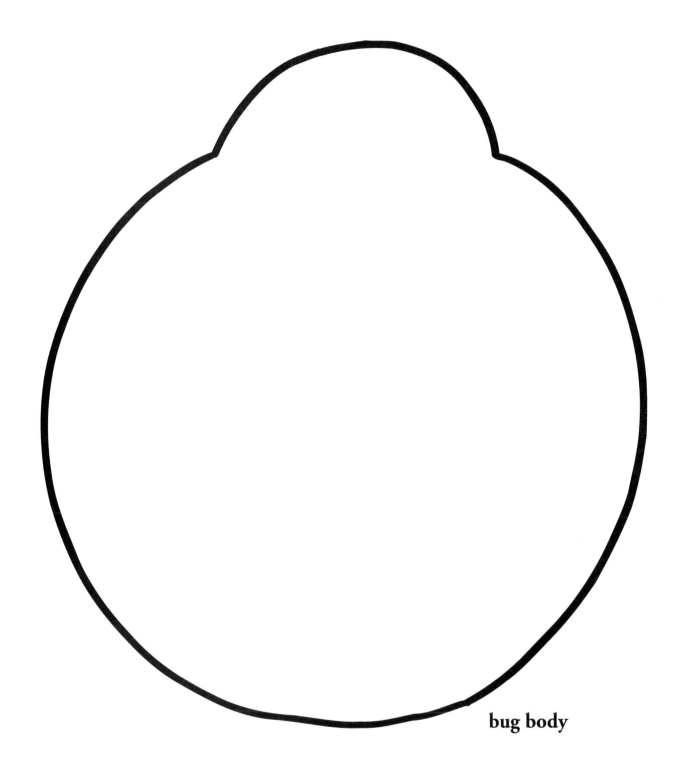

bug body

Questions for Ladybugs

1. What is the fourth book of the Bible? (Numbers)
2. How many days and nights did it rain during the Great Flood? (40 days and 40 nights)
3. How many commandments did God give Moses on Mount Sinai? (10)
4. How many disciples followed Jesus? (12)
5. How many plagues came upon the people of Egypt when they would not let Moses' people go? (10)
6. How many years did the Israelites wander in the wilderness? (40)
7. In what way did the animals come aboard Noah's Ark? (2 by 2)
8. How many tribes were there in Israel? (12)
9. For how many pieces of silver did Judas betray Jesus? (30)
10. How many times did Peter deny Jesus? (3)

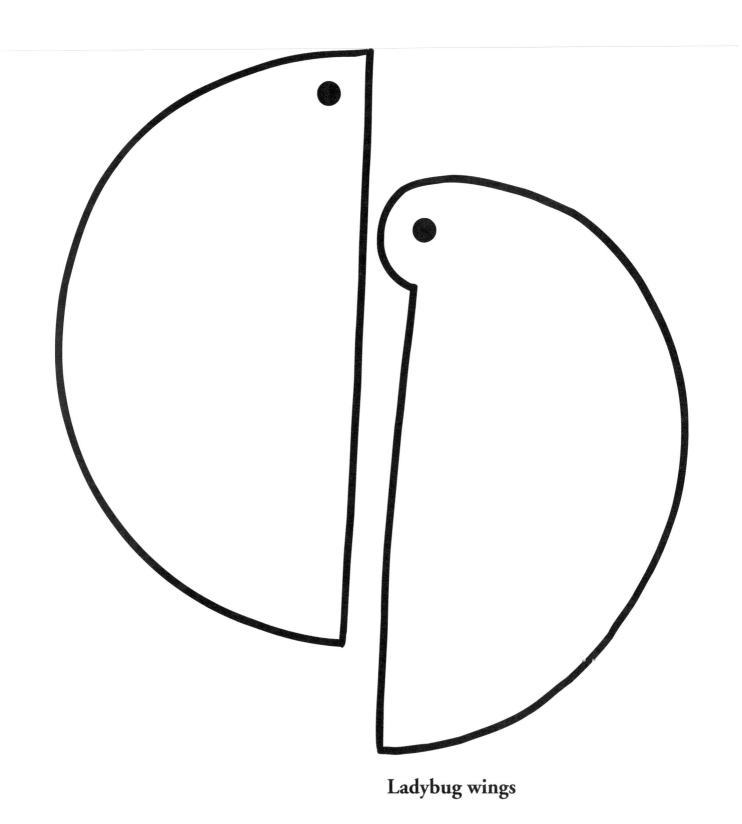

Ladybug wings

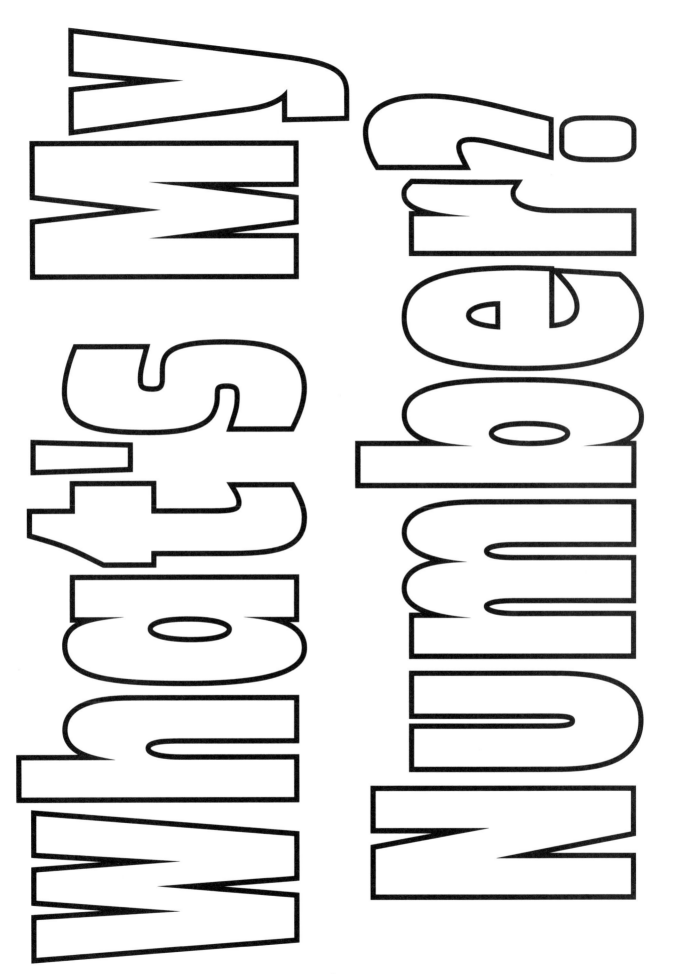

What's My Number?

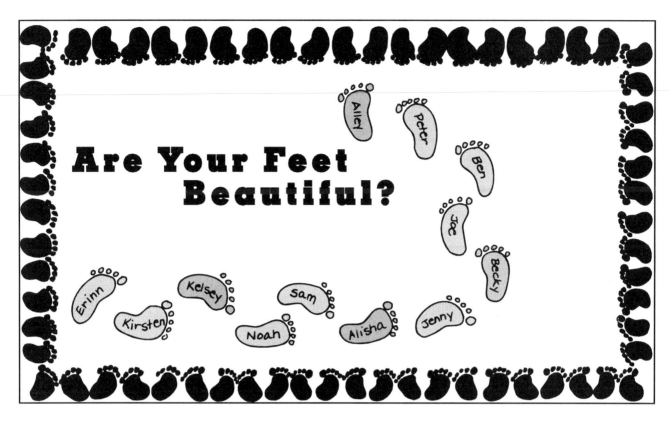

∗ Plan

To realize the call to share God with others.

∗ Memorize

How beautiful…are the feet of those who bring good news. Isaiah 52:7

∗ Gather

- pattern for foot border from p. 11
- pattern for lettering from pp. 81-82
- background paper, green
- construction paper, various colors
- crayons

∗ Prepare

Duplicate the lettering on black construction paper.

∗ Create

1. Attach the green background paper to the bulletin board. Cut out the lettering and post it on the board as shown.
2. Cut and fold strips of black construction paper according to the instant border directions on page 10. Trace the foot border pattern onto the folded paper and cut out the border. Staple the border around the edges of the board.
3. Trace each child's feet onto a piece of construction paper, using a crayon to avoid injury. Use a different color of construction paper for each child if possible. Some of the older children may take turns tracing each other's feet with adult supervision.
4. Cut out the patterns and write the child's name on each foot.
5. Attach the feet to the bulletin board in any pattern desired. You could make them "walk" across the board diagonally or arrange them in a circle. Let your imagination be your guide!

∗ Teach

Cut out one color of feet per child (or groups of children if you have a large class). Place them in different maze patterns—intersecting and reversing—around the room or outside. Have the children follow one color of feet, carrying their Bibles, to act out the memory verse.

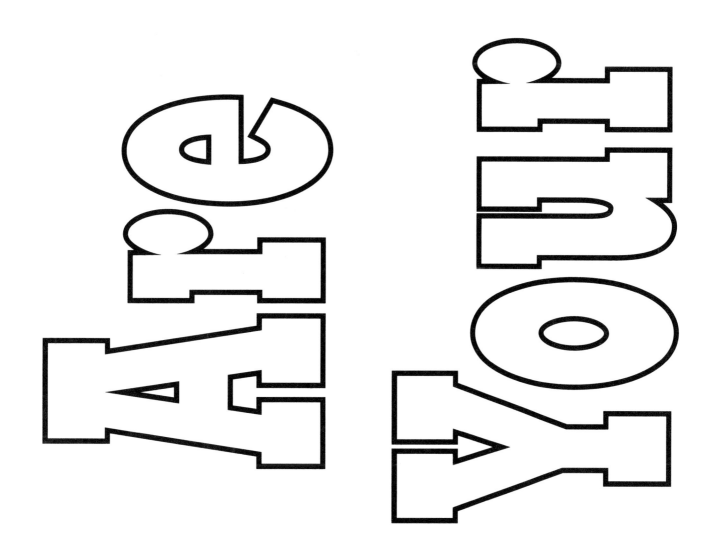

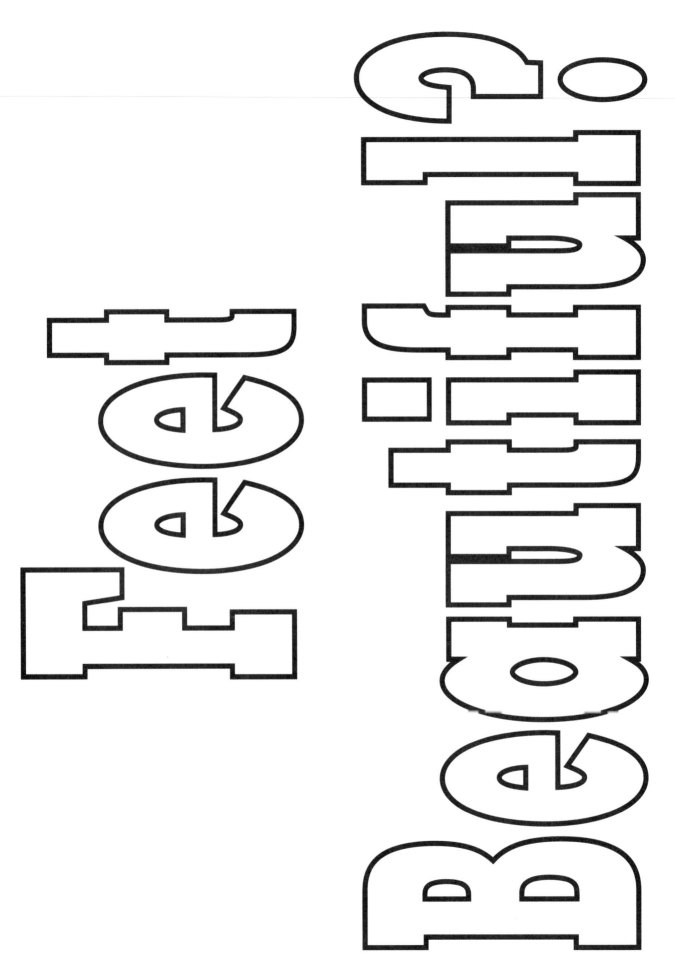

Feet Beautiful

Best Of Friends

There is a friend who sticks closer than a brother.
Proverbs 18:24

Tyler   Andrew   Kim   Erin   Paige   Brittany

✳ Ages 6-10 ✳

✳ Plan
To view God as a best friend.

✳ Memorize
There is a friend who sticks closer than a brother.
Proverbs 18:24

✳ Gather
- pattern for lettering from p. 86
- pattern for heart border from p. 13
- pattern for friends from pp. 84-85
- background paper, black
- construction paper, pink
- paper, white
- crayons
- safety scissors
- chalk, pink and assorted colors

✳ Prepare
Duplicate the lettering on pink construction paper. Duplicate the friend pattern (boy or girl) on white paper, one per child.

✳ Create
1. Cover the bulletin board with the black background paper. Cut out the lettering and attach it to the board as shown. Use pink chalk to write the memory verse at the bottom of the board.

2. Cut and fold strips of pink construction paper according to the instant border directions on page 10. Trace the heart border pattern onto the folded paper and cut out the border. Attach the border around the board's edges.

3. Distribute the friend illustration to each student. Show the students how to fold the pattern sheet and cut the pattern on the solid lines. Have them use crayons to decorate one doll to look like themselves and the other doll to look like their best friend.

4. Attach the dolls to the bulletin board. Have the students write their own name and their friend's name under each doll with different colors of chalk.

✳ Teach
Ask, **What do you like about your best friend?** Give each child an opportunity to share. Then say, **Did you know you have a friend who is better than any best friend you could imagine? God wants to be your best friend. He will always like you, He always tells the truth and He is with you all of the time. Let's thank God for the good friends He has given us, and for the friend He is to us.**

Fold paper on dotted line. Cut out figure using solid black lines as guides. *Do not cut on the fold.* Figures will be holding hands when finished.

Fold paper on dotted line. Cut out figure using solid black lines as guides. *Do not cut on the fold.* Figures will be holding hands when finished.

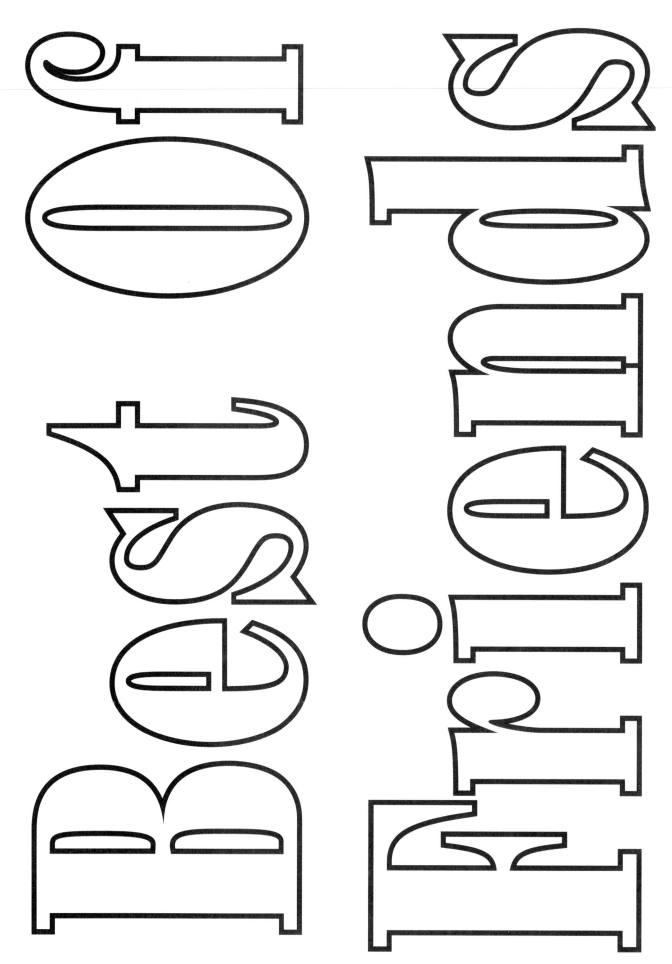

★ Ages 6-10 ★

★ Plan
To learn about godly characteristics.

★ Memorize
The fruit of the Spirit is love, joy, peace, patience, kindness, goodness, faithfulness, gentleness and self-control. Galatians 5:22-23

★ Gather
• pattern for fruit from pp. 88-89
• pattern for lettering from p. 90
• construction paper, black, red, white and assorted colors
• paper plates
• crayons
• safety scissors
• glue

★ Prepare
Cut the red and white construction paper into 4" × 4" squares. Cut the paper plates in half. Duplicate the lettering on black construction paper, and the fruit patterns on white paper.

★ Create
1. Cover the bulletin board with squares of red and white construction paper to make a checkerboard tablecloth. Cut out and attach the lettering as shown.

2. Cut and fold strips of green construction paper according to the border directions on page 88. Trace the grass border pattern onto the folded paper and cut out the border. Attach the border around the board's edges.

3. Provide each student with the fruit patterns and half of a paper plate. Have them use the fruit patterns to trace and cut fruit from colored sheets of construction paper. Instruct them to write the different kinds of spiritual fruit on the front of each (write them on the chalkboard for reference). The students may then color their paper plates brown and write their names on the front.

4. Show how to glue the fruit to the top of the paper plate so that it looks like it is emerging from the bowl. Attach the plates to the bulletin board.

★ Teach
Review each of the fruits of the spirit with the class. Ask, **Which one do you think is the most important? Which one do you think you do best? Which one do you need to improve on? Do you think anyone is perfect at all of these? Only Jesus was perfect. We cannot be Him, but we should try very hard to be like Him.**

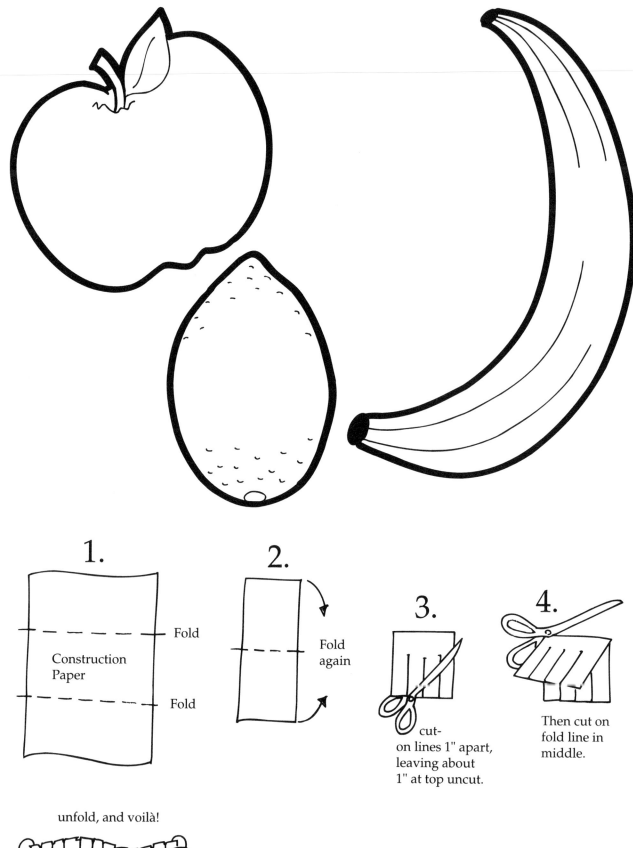

1.

Construction Paper

Fold

Fold

2.

Fold again

3.

cut-
on lines 1" apart,
leaving about
1" at top uncut.

4.

Then cut on
fold line in
middle.

unfold, and voilà!

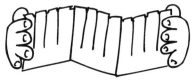

a fringe border!

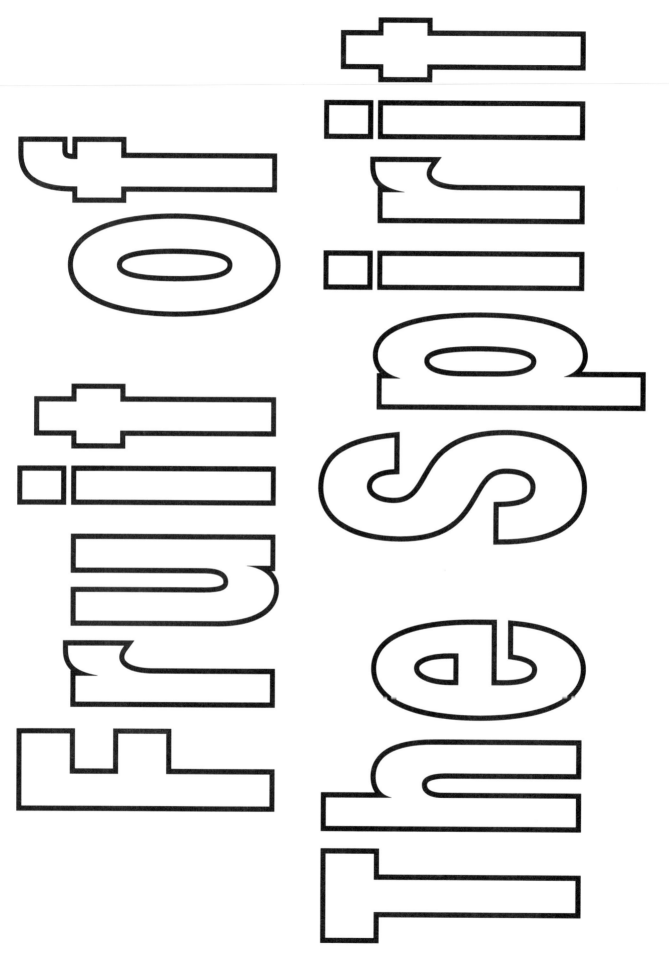

Fruit of The Spirit

* Plan
To affirm that God created a beautiful world.

* Memorize
Perfect in beauty, God shines forth. Psalm 50:2

* Gather
- patterns for camera and booklet cover from pp. 92-93
- pattern for lettering from pp. 94-95
- pattern for checkered border from p. 11
- background paper, yellow
- construction paper, black and various colors
- camera
- magazines
- glue stick
- safety scissors
- tape

* Prepare
Duplicate the lettering on black construction paper. Duplicate the camera and booklet cover on white paper, one set per child. Cut out the cameras. Fold the booklet covers in half with the cover on the front, then fold and staple various colors of construction paper pages inside. Cover the staples with tape to avoid scratching.

* Create
1. Attach the yellow background paper to the bulletin board. Cut out the lettering and post it as shown.

2. Cut and fold strips of black construction paper according to the instant border directions on page 10. Trace the checkered border pattern onto the folded paper and cut out the border. Staple the border around the edges of the board.

3. Give each child a camera to color. Write the students' names on their cameras and attach the cameras to the board.

4. Have the children look through old magazines for pictures of landscapes or animals and cut them out.

5. Show how to glue the pictures in the booklet with a glue stick.

6. Attach the booklets to the bulletin board near each child's camera.

* Teach
Discuss the things in the pictures that God created. As you go through them, say, **God created the cows perfect in beauty; God created the chickens perfect in beauty, etc.** Have the children make the sounds that represent the pictures they have cut out. Say, **God's world is beautiful, isn't it? That is because God is perfect and beautiful. He created the beautiful world just for us because He loves us so much.**

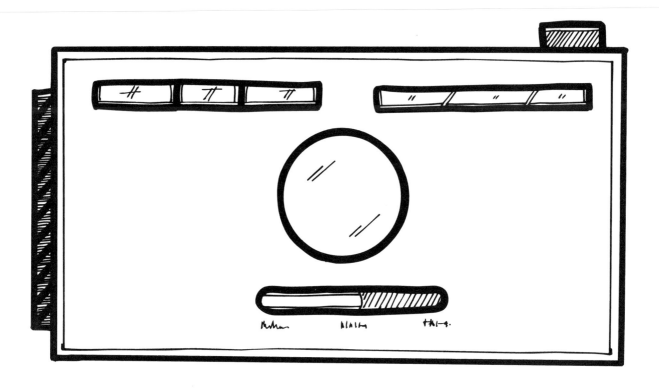

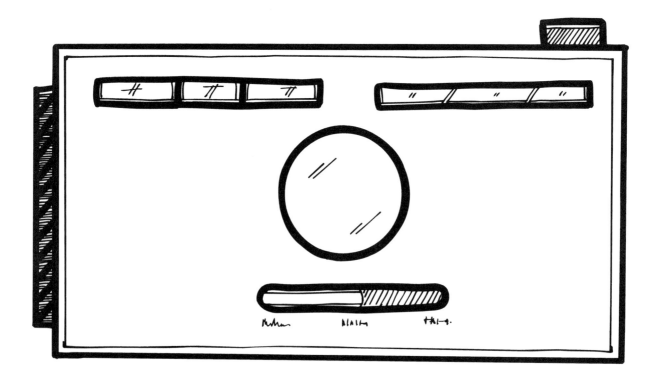

Book of

_____'s

God's Perfect
Things

God Makes Picture

94

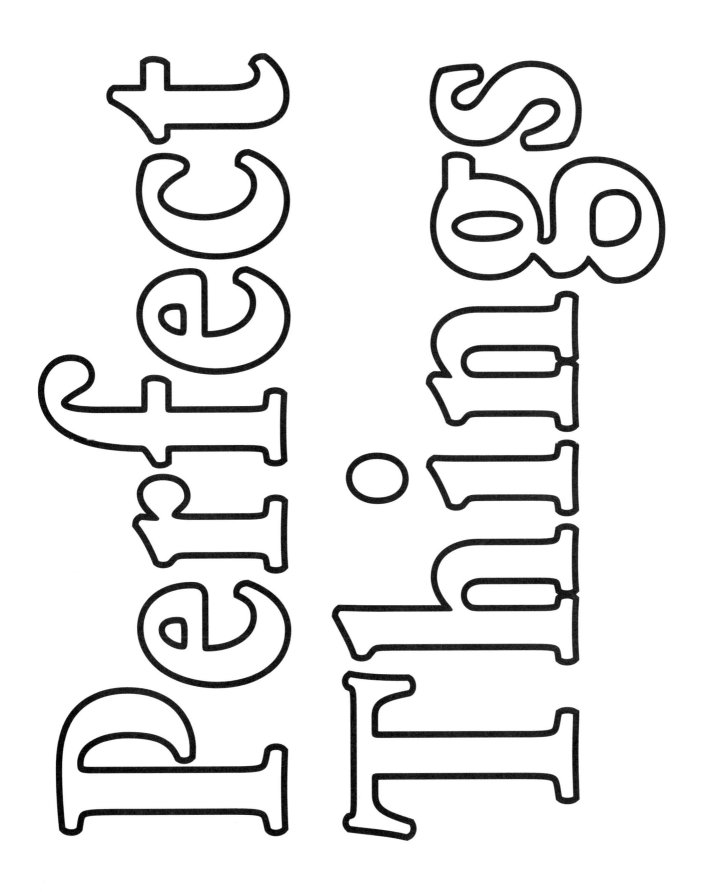

Perfect Things

* Plan

To explain what happens to Believers.

* Memorize

Whoever believes in me, as the Scripture has said, streams of living water will flow from within him.
John 7:38

* Gather

- patterns for sailboat from pp. 97-98
- pattern for wave border from p. 13
- pattern for lettering from p. 99
- background paper, light blue and dark blue or green
- construction paper, white, yellow and red
- crayons
- clear, self-stick plastic
- Velcro
- plastic sandwich bag, large
- push pin

* Prepare

Duplicate the lettering on white construction paper. Trace the sailboat hulls on red construction paper, the sails on white construction paper (two per boat), the pennants on yellow construction paper and the masts on brown construction paper—making enough for 19 boats. Cut out the boat pieces.

* Create

1. Cover the bulletin board with the light blue background paper. For the bottom ⅓ of the board, attach dark blue or green paper cut into waves. Cut out the lettering and attach it to the board as shown.

2. Cut and fold strips of yellow construction paper according to the instant border directions on page 10. Trace the wave border pattern onto the folded paper and cut out the border. Staple the border around the board's edges.

3. Have the students help you to arrange and glue the boat parts together as shown.

4. Collect the boats and write one word of the memory verse on each. Cover the boats with clear, self-stick plastic for durability.

5. Place small pieces of Velcro on the bulletin board and their corresponding pieces on the backs of the boats. Store the boats in a large plastic sandwich bag attached with a push pin to the bottom right corner of the board.

6. Invite the students to discover the mystery verse by arranging the boats in the correct verse order.

* Teach

Read the memory verse to the class. Ask, **Who is talking in this verse? Do you think Jesus meant that water will come gushing out of your physical heart if you believe in Him? Of course not. What does Jesus mean? What do we have to do to show that we believe in Him?**

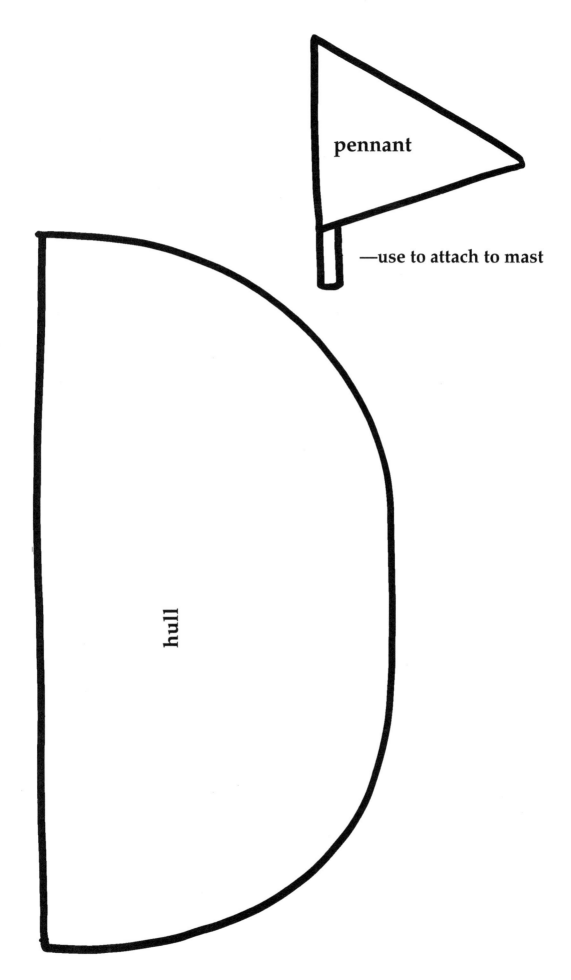

pennant

—use to attach to mast

hull

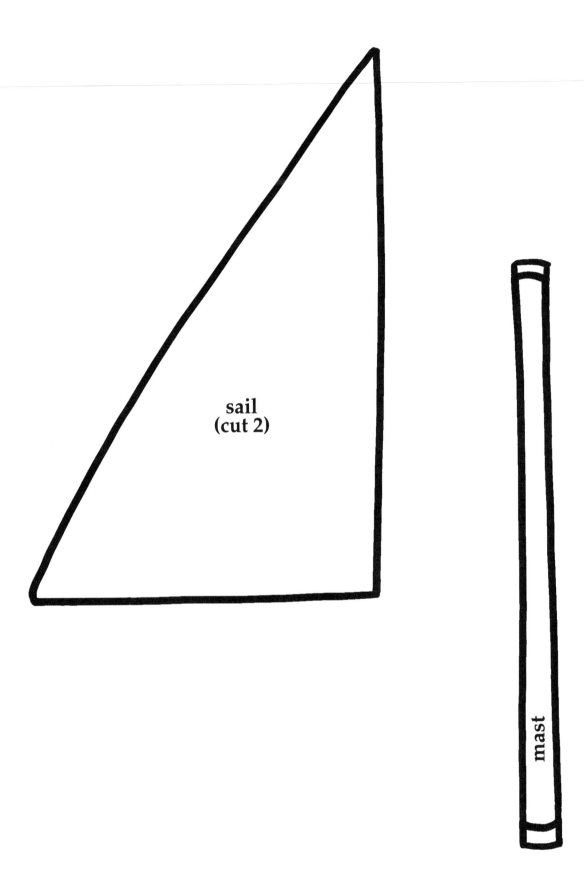

sail
(cut 2)

mast

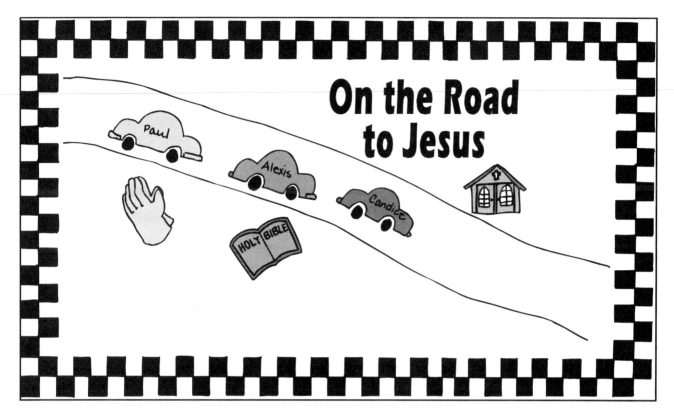

* Ages 2-5 *

* Plan
To understand the journey of life.

* Memorize
Small is the gate and narrow the road that leads to life. Matthew 7:14

* Gather
- pattern for lettering from p. 105
- pattern for checkered border from p. 11
- patterns for praying hands, Bible, church and cars from pp. 101-104
- background paper, green
- felt, gray
- construction paper, various colors
- sandpaper
- glue
- crayons

* Prepare
Duplicate the lettering on black construction paper, and the praying hands, Bible and church patterns on white paper. Duplicate the car on various colors of construction paper, one per child.

* Create
1. Attach the green background paper to the board. Cut out the lettering and post it on the board as shown.
2. Cut and fold strips of black construction paper according to the instant border directions on page 10. Trace the checkered border pattern onto the folded paper and cut out the border. Staple the border around the edges of the board.
3. Cut out a gray felt "road" and staple it to the bulletin board as shown.
4. Cut out the cars. Write a child's name on each car and glue a small piece of sandpaper to the back of each one.
5. Cut out the praying hands, Bible and church. Color or decorate all three pieces. Attach the items to each side of the felt road.
6. The children may move their cars along the felt road.

* Teach
Ask, **Who is going on a trip this summer?** Allow the children an opportunity to tell you about their vacation plans. Say, **There is one long trip you are always on and that is the journey of your life with Jesus. He is with us all of the way, but we can make the trip a lot better if we pray, read our Bibles and go to church. Move your car on the bulletin board and make sure you stop at the right times for prayer, reading the Bible and church. What a nice trip you will have!**

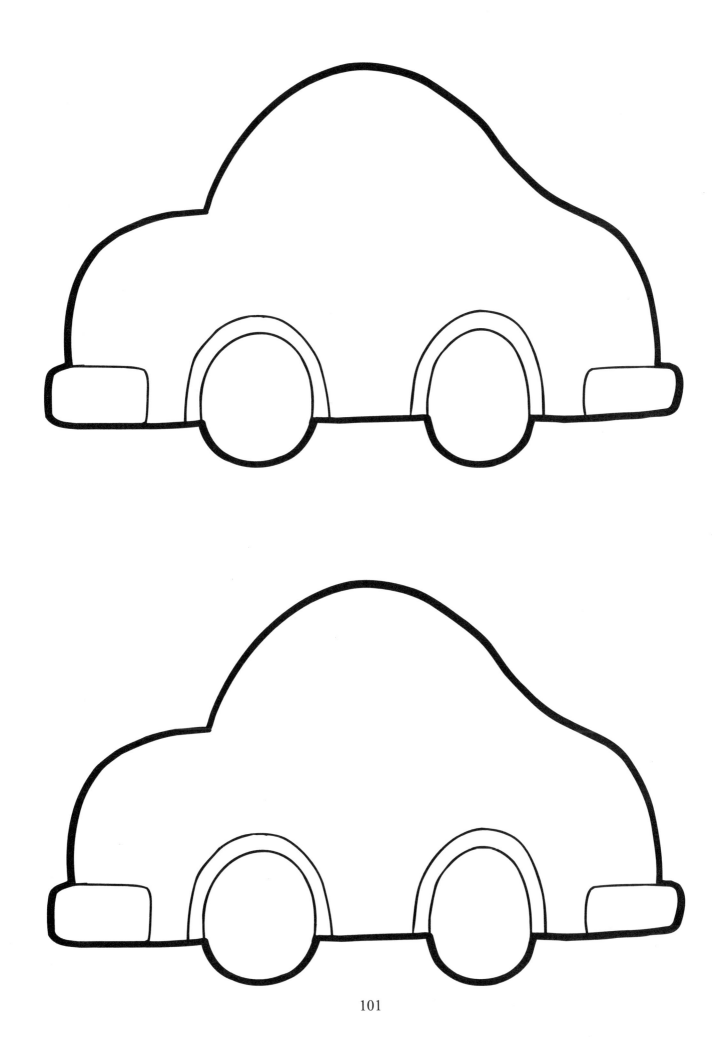

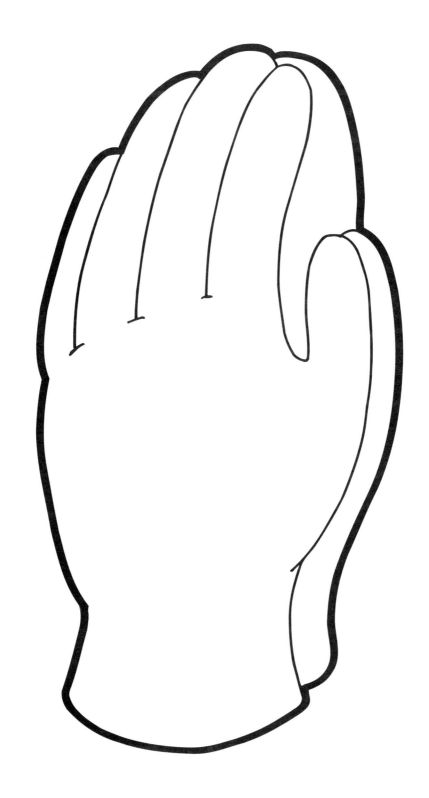

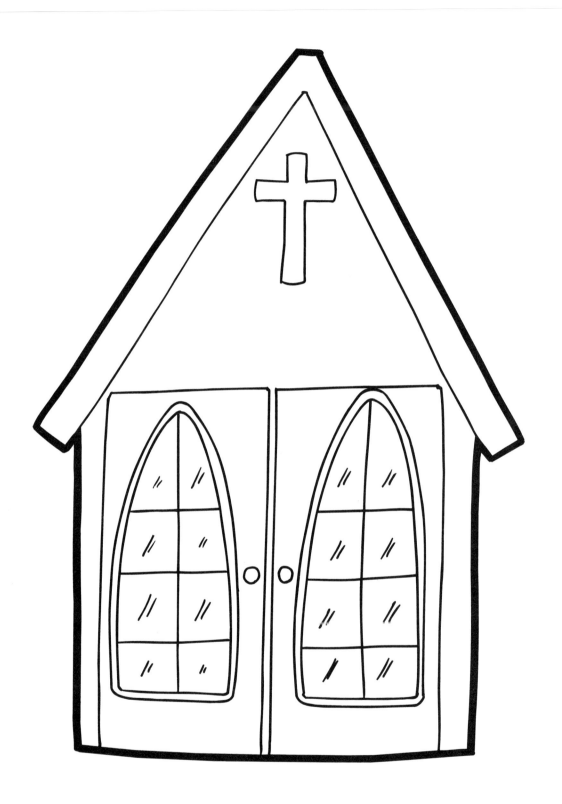

the to

On Road Jesus

Let us run with perseverance the race marked out for us. Hebrews 12:1

✳ Ages 6-10 ✳

✳ Plan
To understand the goal in life is to help other people know God.

✳ Memorize
Let us run with perseverance the race marked out for us. Hebrews 12:1

✳ Gather
- pattern for trophy from p. 107
- pattern for trophy border from p. 12
- pattern for lettering from p. 108
- background paper, green
- aluminum foil
- marker, black
- poster board
- pencils
- safety scissors
- glue
- glitter and faux jewels

✳ Prepare
Trace the lettering on aluminum foil. Duplicate the trophy on white paper, one per student.

✳ Create
1. Cover the bulletin board with green background paper. Cut out the lettering and attach it to the board as shown. Use a black marker to write the Bible verse at the bottom of the board.

2. Cut and fold strips of aluminum foil according to the instant border directions on page 10. Trace the trophy border pattern onto the folded paper and cut out the border. Attach the border around the board's edges.

3. Distribute the trophies to the students. Have them cut out and use the pattern to trace and cut out a trophy from poster board. Instruct the students to cover their trophies with aluminum foil. They may decorate the trophies with glitter or faux jewels.

4. Attach the trophies to the bulletin board.

✳ Teach
Lead the students in a variety of races to illustrate the memory verse. Some ideas: frog jump, sack relay, two-person wheelbarrow, hop on one foot, etc. Remind the students that the race to tell others about Jesus is the most important race to run.

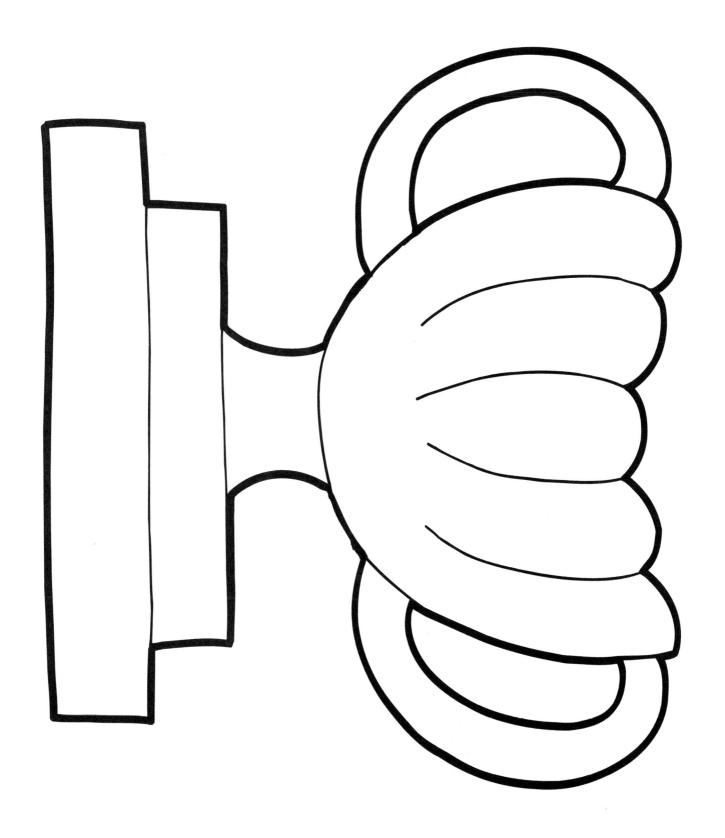

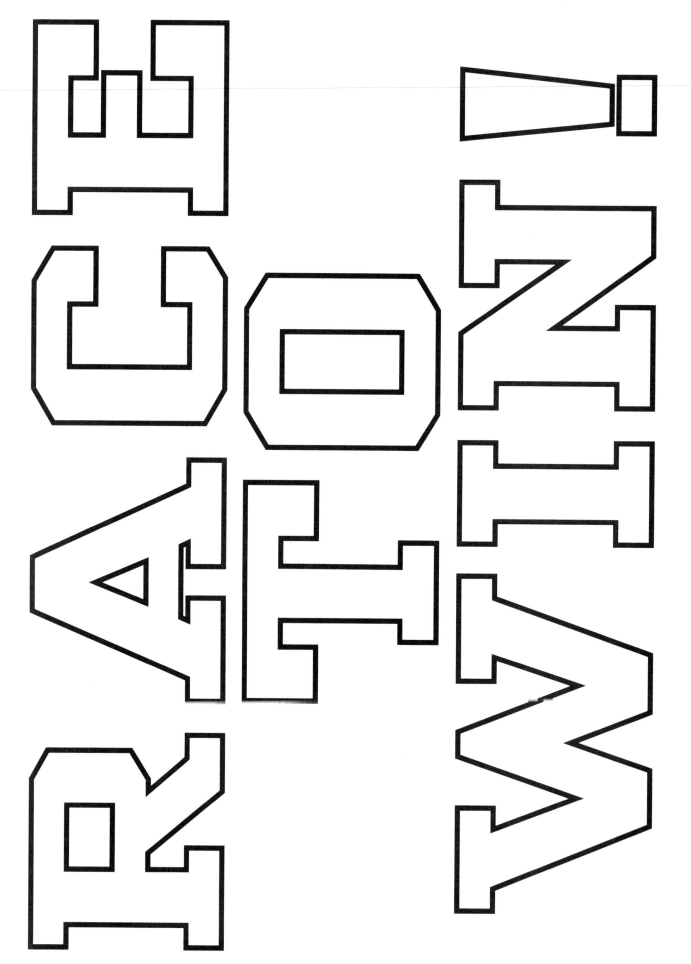

Therefore go and make disciples of all nations. Matthew 28:19

✳ Ages 6-10 ✳

✳ Plan
To emphasize the importance of sharing the Good News.

✳ Memorize
Therefore go and make disciples of all nations.
Matthew 28:19

✳ Gather
- pattern for people border from p. 12
- pattern for lettering from pp. 111-112
- pattern for figurine from p. 110
- background paper, light blue
- poster paper, white
- tempera paint, blue, green and brown
- paint brush
- construction paper, purple
- marker, black
- encyclopedias
- fabric or construction paper scraps
- glue
- crayons
- safety scissors

✳ Prepare
Duplicate the lettering on purple construction paper. Duplicate one figurine for each child.

✳ Create
1. Cover the bulletin board with the light blue background paper.
2. Make the earth in the center of the board by painting green and brown land forms on a large circle of blue poster paper (see illustration above). Allow to dry, then attach it to the center of the bulletin board.
3. Cut out the lettering and attach it to the board as shown. Use a black marker to write the Bible verse at the bottom of the board.
4. Cut and fold strips of purple construction paper according to the instant border directions on page 10. Trace the people border pattern onto the folded paper and cut out the border. Attach the border around the board's edges.
5. Distribute the figures to the students and allow them to cut one out. Have each child select a country and research it in an encyclopedia. Ask the students to decorate their figures to match the native dress of that country (you may want to provide fabric scraps and glue).
6. Attach the figures to the bulletin board as shown.

✳ Teach
Bring foods representing different countries for the children to taste while they work on this project (nachos and salsa, rice, French bread, etc.). Also bring a photocopied page from a plain calendar. After the children have selected a country for their figures, write their chosen countries on the days your class will meet. Then commit with the students to pray for the children in each country on the designated Sundays.

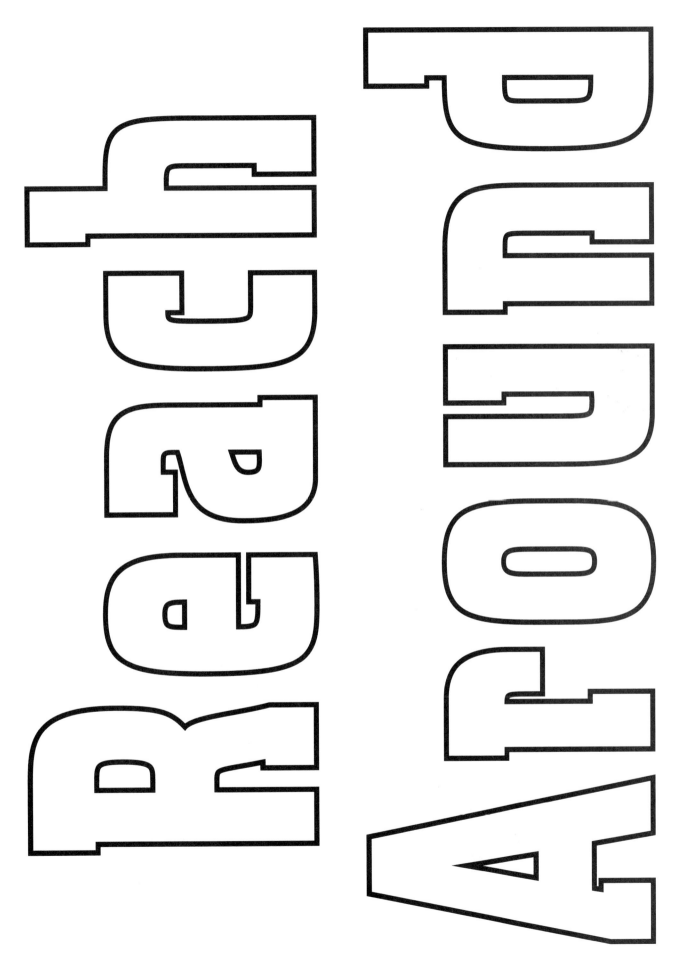

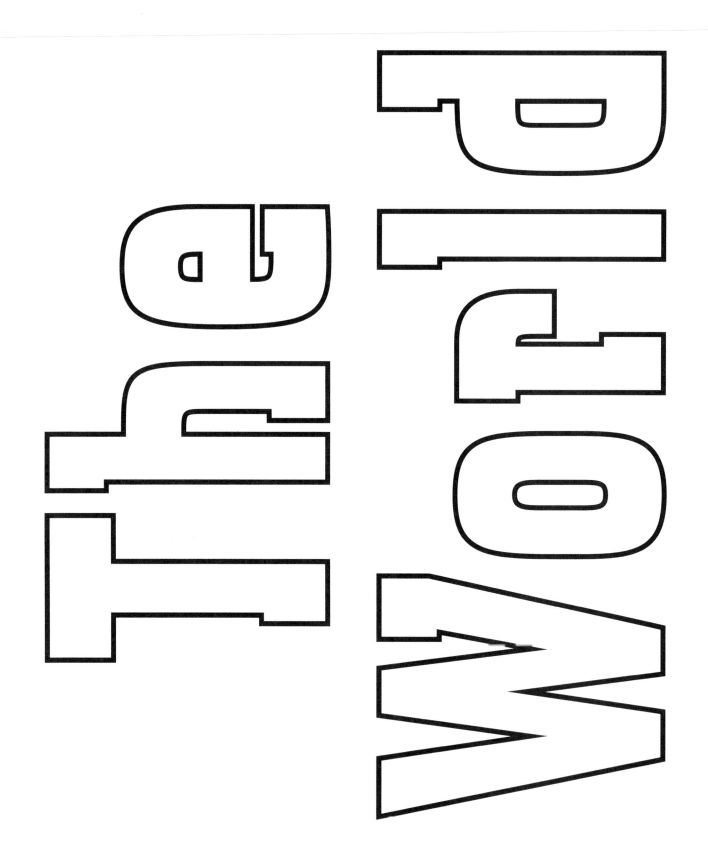

For wisdom is more precious than rubies, and nothing you desire can compare with her. Proverbs 8:11

✳ Ages 6-10 ✳

✳ Plan
To explain that true wisdom comes from God.

✳ Memorize
For wisdom is more precious than rubies, and nothing you desire can compare with her. Proverbs 8:11

✳ Gather
• pattern for gems from pp. 114-116
• pattern for gem border from p. 14
• pattern for lettering from p. 117
• background paper, black
• glitter, mixed colors
• glue
• foil, silver and red
• Bibles
• crayons
• safety scissors

✳ Prepare
Duplicate the gems on white paper. Trace the lettering on silver foil and cut out.

✳ Create
1. Cover the bulletin board with the black background paper. Post the lettering as shown across the top of the board. "Write" the memory verse with glue and sprinkle with glitter. Allow to dry. (You may want to do the memory verse on a separate sheet of black paper and attach it to the board after it dries.)

2. Cut and fold strips of red foil according to the instant border directions on page 10. Trace the gem border pattern onto the folded paper and cut out the border. Attach the border around the board's edges.

3. Distribute the gems, crayons and scissors to the students. Discuss several verses from Proverbs with the class, including the memory verse. Ask the students to look up and write their favorite Proverbs verse and their names on their gems, then color and cut them out. They may select more than one gem if they have several favorite verses.

4. Attach the gems to the bulletin board.

✳ Teach
Before beginning this project, share a story about Solomon's wisdom from the Bible or a Bible story book. Children especially enjoy the story of the baby with two mothers from 1 Kings, chapter 3. Say, **Books and education make us wise and they are good and right. But where can we go for wisdom when we really need it? How can we talk to Him? How do we know He will hear us?**

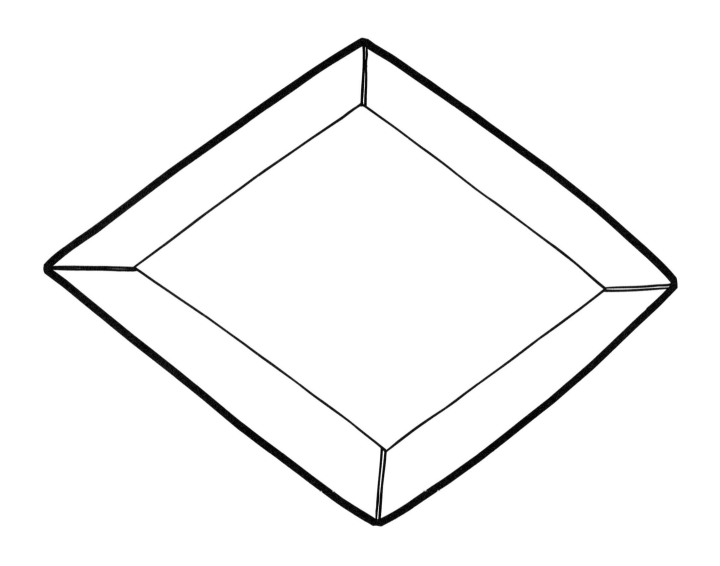

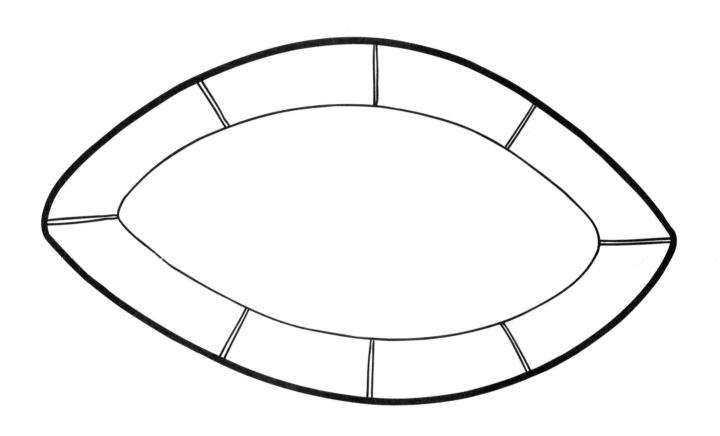

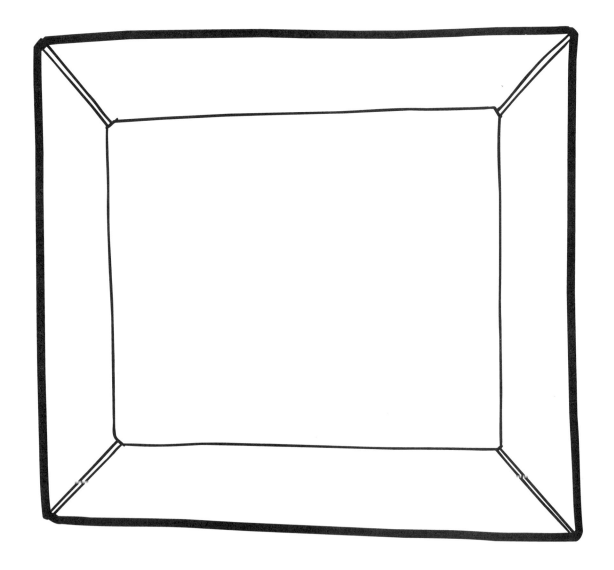

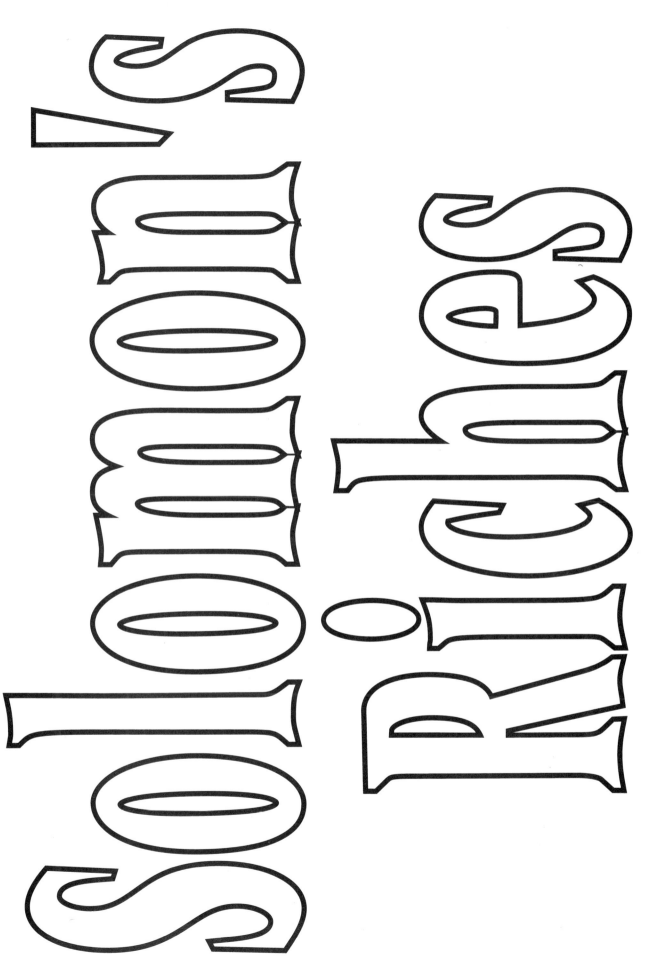

Tell It Like It Is!

I will proclaim the name of the Lord.
Deuteronomy 32:3

(T-shirt messages shown: "I am A X-tian", "He is King!", "Jesus is the Way!", "GOD is LOVE", "I ♥ Jesus", "Praise the Lord!")

* **Ages 6-10** *

* Plan
To affirm the students' responsibility to be witnesses.

* Memorize
I will proclaim the name of the Lord.
Deuteronomy 32:3

* Gather
• pattern for lettering from p. 120
• pattern for T-shirt from p. 119
• pattern for shirt border from p. 14
• background paper, orange
• construction paper, black and white
• crayons
• safety scissors
• fabric pens, glitter, beads (optional)

* Prepare
Duplicate the lettering on black construction paper. Duplicate the T-shirt pattern on white construction paper, one per child.

* Create
1. Cover the bulletin board with brightly colored background paper. Cut out the lettering and attach it to the board as shown. Use a black marker to write the Bible verse on the board.
2. Cut and fold strips of white construction paper according to the instant border directions on page 10. Trace the shirt border pattern onto the folded paper and cut out the border. Attach the border around the board's edges.
3. Distribute the T-shirts, crayons and scissors to the students. Discuss the different kinds of "witness wear" shirts the students have seen and how people use T-shirts to communicate ideas with each other (bring in some samples, if available.) Have the students color and cut out their own message T-shirts.
4. Attach the shirts to the bulletin board.

* Teach
Make wearable Christian T-shirts with your class to match your bulletin board. Have the students bring in a plain, white T-shirt. Supply fabric pens and other decorations for T-shirts, such as glitter, glue-on appliqués, beads, etc. Challenge the students to use their creativity—have everyone vote on "prettiest," "most creative," "best message," etc., after all have finished.

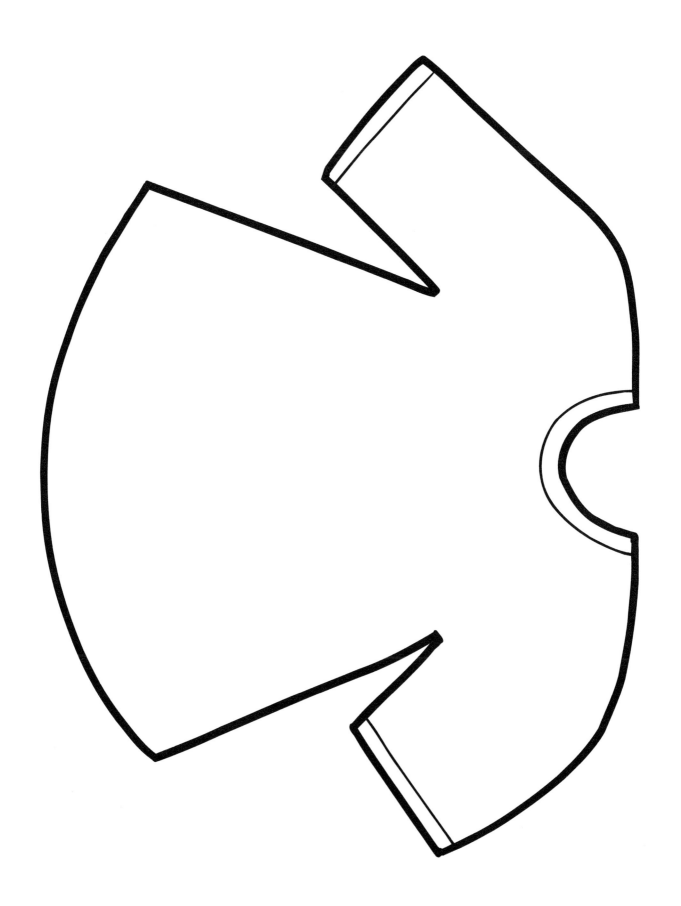

120

✳ Ages 2-5 ✳

✳ Plan

To reinforce that God gives us talents to use for Him.

✳ Memorize

Do it all for the glory of God.
1 Corinthians 10:31

✳ Gather

• pattern for lettering from p. 128
• pattern for diamond border from p. 13
• patterns for heads and hats from pp. 122-127
• background paper, red
• paper, white
• Velcro
• scissors
• crayons

✳ Prepare

Duplicate the lettering on white construction paper, and the heads and hats on white paper.

✳ Create

1. Attach the red background paper to the bulletin board. Cut out the lettering and post it as shown.
2. Cut and fold strips of white construction paper according to the instant border directions on page 10. Trace the diamond border pattern onto the folded paper and cut out the border. Staple the border around the edges of the board.
3. Cut out the heads and hats. Color the illustrations.
4. Attach the heads to the bulletin board. Be sure to leave enough space between the heads for the hats.
5. Attach a piece of Velcro to each hat and the corresponding piece to the board above each head.
6. Invite the children to move the hats from one person to another.

✳ Teach

Say, **Is there any correct way to place the hats? Not really, is there? Any of these people could be a nurse, a policeman, a professor or a chef — just like any of you could be anything you want to be. Isn't it great that God gives each of us different kinds of talents?** Point out a special ability that each child has (artistic, musical, friendly, etc.). Say, **We should remember to always praise God for our talents and to use them for His glory, like the memory verse says.**

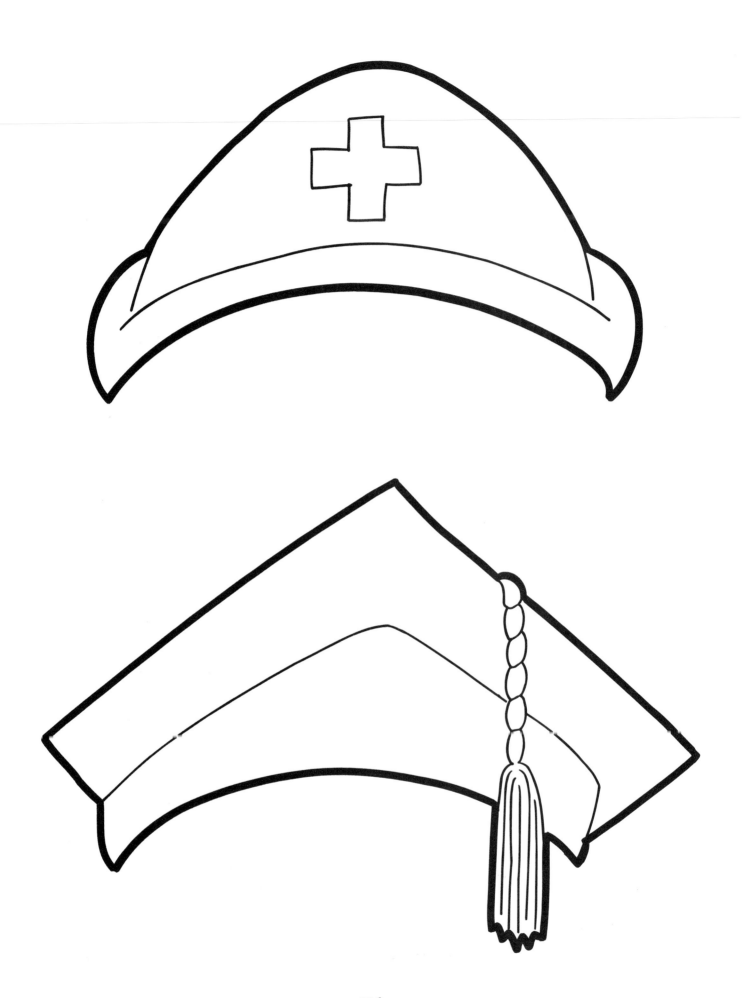

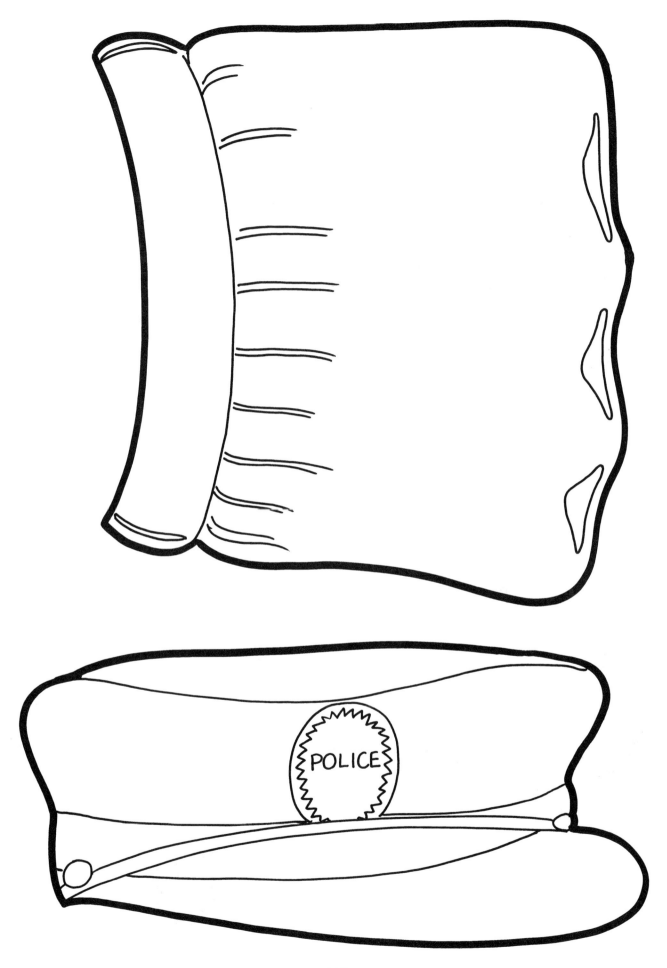